WILD COURAGE

This is my favorit
business book!
Unfortunately, it's out
of print but you'll
see it's an amazing
mix of business and
spirituality.
(in a good way!)

Hope you'll enjoy
it.

            francois

Elle Harrison is founder of Wild Courage (www.wildcourage.com) where she consults internationally as a Leadership Coach and workshop facilitator. Her passion is guiding leaders and organizations through change, to find purpose and meaning in their work and to uncover creative solutions to the social and environmental challenges of our time.

Elle began her career with Unilever, working in global innovation and marketing in the UK, Thailand and Argentina. In 2004, she quit corporate life to embark on her own journey of transformation, following her curiosity across cultures, continents and philosophies to learn about intuition, creativity, transformation and the human soul. Her coaching, workshops and talks draw on the richness and diversity of these perspectives, creating soulful, challenging and transformational experiences for individuals and organizations.

She is a Professional Certified Coach with the International Coach Federation, has trained as a Wilderness Rites of Passage Guide with the School of Lost Borders, and has a degree from Cambridge University, England.

Elle lives in London, England and spends several months of the year in Northern California. She can be reached on elle@wildcourage.com.

WILD COURAGE

*A Journey of Transformation
for you and your business*

Elle Harrison

WATKINS PUBLISHING

LONDON

This edition first published in the UK and USA 2011 by
Watkins Publishing, Sixth Floor, Castle House,
75–76 Wells Street, London W1T 3QH

1 3 5 7 9 10 8 6 4 2

Designed by Jerry Goldie

Printed and bound by Imago in China

British Library Cataloguing-in-Publication Data Available

Library of Congress Cataloging-in-Publication Data Available

ISBN: 978-1-907486-91-3

www.watkinspublishing.co.uk

Distributed in the USA and Canada by Sterling Publishing Co., Inc.
387 Park Avenue South, New York, NY 10016-8810

For information about custom editions, special sales, premium and
corporate purchases, please contact Sterling Special Sales
Department at 800-805-5489 or specialsales@sterlingpub.com

Contents

You have been telling the people that this
is the Eleventh Hour.
Now you must go back and tell the people that this
is The Hour.
And there are things to be considered.

Where are you living?
What are you doing?
What are your relationships? Are you in right relation?
Where is your water? Know your garden.
It is time to speak your Truth.
Create your community. Be good to each other.
And do not look outside yourself for the leader.

This could be a good time.

At this time in history we are able to take nothing personally,
least of all, ourselves.
The time of the lone wolf is over. Gather yourselves!
Banish the word struggle from your attitude and your vocabulary.
All that we do now must be done in a sacred manner
and in celebration.

There is a river flowing now very fast.
It is so great and swift,
that there are those who will be afraid.
They will try to hold on to the shore.
They will feel they are being torn apart and will suffer greatly.
Know the river has its destination.

The elders say we must let go of the shore,
push off into the middle of the river,
keep our eyes open and our heads above the water.
And I say: see who is in there with you and celebrate.

We are the ones we have been waiting for.

– ELDERS OF THE HOPI NATION, ORAIBI, ARIZONA

Foreword

Before writing this foreword, I thought I'd do a little homework. So I did a search on amazon.com. I entered the search phrase 'leadership and management'. The site returned exactly 18,721 entries for books relevant to that topic. Amazing. While I have to admit that I did not examine all 18,721 entries, I did peruse the top 30 or so. It turns out that I have a number of those books on my shelf. For years, especially when I was a very visible CEO of a public company, publishers, authors, and colleagues sent them to me, gratis, for comments or because they thought they represented serious breakthroughs of one kind or another. Many of the books introduced a chic new terminology that got integrated into the mainstream, got talked about and, for a while, added to the excitement of management and leadership. And then, inevitably, the collective buzz trailed off. I have to admit that I stopped reading or even scanning these 'break-through' books quite some time ago. I know that the core concepts in many of them actually are valid and relevant to prospective leaders. But, all too often, it seems to me that they just recycle the same 'Management 101' concepts that those of us who have been building and operating businesses at scale were taught a long time ago. What's more, I have long had a suspicion that these authors are leaving important things out. Things that everyone knows are hard to deal with. But important.

Wild Courage is different. I was honored when Elle asked me to write a Foreword. And, when I read her first draft, I got excited because it became clear that she was attempting to turn much of the classic thought about leadership on its head. Elle shares what I think is a profound insight: that maybe, just maybe, some of the things that old-school teachings urged aspiring leaders and managers to avoid are the very things that can bring real power to our leadership and work.

I've had a long and fortunate career building successful businesses. Very early on, I was taught all the classic tenets and conventional wisdom of leadership. Yet I've spent my professional life embracing change, not avoiding it, and I have experienced firsthand the power of innovation. When true innovation happens, it is almost always because some great entrepreneur decides to use the very thing that established players consider counterintuitive or actually avoid. It is also almost always the case that the counterintuitive thing is criticized by conventional thinkers. Hindsight is a great thing, and, in hindsight, the new way always looks obvious. But it seldom appears that way at the beginning. Elle might not think of herself as an entrepreneur, but this book marks her out as one. The message is clear: embrace change and lead from the heart with courage and honesty.

Beyond the call to personal change, *Wild Courage* also points to a fundamental change that I believe is underway in the world. At least I hope it is a fundamental and lasting change. It seems to me that, especially in the current atmosphere of crisis, uncertainty, and fear, citizens of the world are desperately hungry for a truthfulness, clarity, candor, and, most important, authenticity that they have not gotten from their leaders in a very long time. In my opinion, they are right to be asking for these things. And through the journey of transformation that it offers, *Wild Courage* challenges and guides us to integrate these qualities into our way of living and leading.

In my opinion, this book is brave, timely, and right on point. The work that Elle challenges us to do is not easy. But it is essential. And, if you have the courage to live and lead with authenticity, it may lead you to a level of impact, purpose and joy you might not have thought possible.

Enjoy!

Tim Koogle, Founding CEO of Yahoo!

Introduction

And the day came when the risk to remain tight in a bud
was more painful than the risk it took to blossom.

– ANAIS NIN –

Sometimes we come to a place where the old ways no longer work. Attitudes and behaviours that generated success in the past no longer get the results we want. Accolades, challenges and achievements that once made us proud no longer fill us up. Strategies for growth no longer deliver results. Brands and businesses that once thrived now limp along, failing to inspire the people they serve or employ. Somehow, without any logical explanation, the 'success formula' that worked so reliably in the past simply stops working. And we know, like it or not, it's time for change.

This call for change can show up in any number of ways. Sometimes it comes screeching into our lives, loud and flamboyant: our team or company goes through a major reorganization, the market crashes, sales plummet, or illness or loss in our personal lives turns our world upside down, sending ripples of change out across every aspect of our life and work. Other times the call to change is more subtle: a quiet, unshakable sense that we're wasting our lives, that there is something 'more', that we are not fulfilling our true potential, that we have somehow taken a path that looks good but fundamentally lacks passion, purpose and meaning. Or the changes simply seep into our world through a quiet yet powerful intuition that the world is changing, and that we need to adapt as leaders and businesses to be compelling and sustainable in our emerging world.

What do we do when we hear this call for change? Often, we bury our head in the sand and hope it will go away. No sane human being walks into the fires of transformation without good reason – we know the perils and challenges of that journey too well to engage with it lightly. So we close our ears, dig in our heels, and continue what we've been doing with renewed vigour. We try harder and harder and harder, applying the old, familiar approaches that worked so well for us in the past. Meanwhile, in an effort to tranquilize the call for transformation, we might make surface changes. As leaders, we might take on a new role; as organizations we might restructure, develop new systems and processes, modify our sourcing strategy, move offices or adapt our product offering. This kind of surface change may work for some time, yet ultimately, it is rarely enough to satisfy the deeper demand for change.

True transformation asks much more of us. It asks us to change deeply, from the inside out. To change not only what we are doing, but also who we are being; not only the actions we take, but also the lens through which we see the world. It asks us to go deep within our selves to dissolve old perspectives, so that we can put things back together in wholly new and creative ways. To die to the past, and to who we have been in the past, to make space for who we are becoming – as leaders, organizations and communities. Transformation asks us to leave behind the solid ground of our old reality, and to step onto a shifting and uncertain surface towards an unknown future. This is a challenging and often terrifying task, and it requires great courage.

My first encounter with this kind of transformational journey came in 2004, when I left a successful global career in marketing for Unilever, and set out into the unknown. It took several years of patiently following my curiosity to finally emerge on new ground, in a new career – supporting leaders and organizations through change with my own company, Wild Courage.

Over the last seven years, in my role as Leadership Coach, I've witnessed and guided hundreds of leaders through similar periods of change and transition. In that time, I've been privileged to work with a wide range of leaders. Some are CEOs and senior executives who tick all the boxes of 'success': highly regarded in their profession, influential, well paid, with a happy family life, yet wondering: *is this it?* Others are earlier in their careers, in their late 20s and early 30s, high achievers looking down the path of 'success' and asking: *is this really how I want to spend the next thirty years of my life?* Others hold no formal leadership position, but are leaders in a broader sense – creating impact in the world through art, parenting, voluntary work and relationships. All of them share a longing to make a difference, to contribute something of value and to live a full and authentic life; all of them are willing to engage in a journey of transformation to stay true to this longing.

Over the years, as I guided these different leaders through change, I began to notice similarities in their experiences. Each journey of transformation was unique, triggered by different circumstances and leading to distinct personal challenges. Yet, within these differences, I also started to recognize certain patterns. Somehow, regardless of where their journeys began, all these leaders faced experiences that brought them face to face with the same six qualities. These were: **Dying, Stillness, Intuition, Wildness, Vulnerability and Surrender.**

It seemed that, regardless of where their journey began, it consistently led them to experiences with these six human qualities. In a sense, an encounter with each of these qualities became a threshold to take them deeper into their journey of transformation. Dying to old habits and identities created space for something new to emerge. It led them into an empty, in-between space where they learned to trust Stillness and wait attentively and patiently for the new world to take form. Intuition offered guidance through the murkiness of change, leading the way into new possibilities and new life. Wildness helped them break free of old rules, beliefs and habits that were limiting their creativity and authenticity. Vulnerability, the willingness to feel and share feelings, created a deeper sense of trust and community. And Surrender? Surrender was the current running through all these qualities. Letting go of the need to control and direct life opened the way for radically new solutions to emerge.

Curiously, we don't usually associate these six qualities with successful leaders and businesses. In fact, they are qualities that we traditionally overlook, dismiss or even judge. Dying (decline and endings) is seen as a failure. Stillness is considered a waste of time. Intuition is a gamble, only to be trusted when backed up with rational arguments and concrete data. Wildness is an act of rebellion that makes us dangerous and ultimately unemployable. Vulnerability is weakness that no leader should expose. Surrender, with the loss of control it suggests, is not even part of our vocabulary. So it may be surprising to discover that the path of transformation winds through these forgotten and little-loved aspects of life and leadership.

Yet, traditional wisdom and mythology has always taught us that growth comes from venturing into new and unfamiliar terrain. Twentieth-century mythologist Joseph Campbell studied myths across time to create a map of the journey into mature leadership. He called it the Hero's Journey, and outlined three clear, consistent elements: the hero leaves the familiarity of his home, embarks on a wild and dangerous adventure that opens him to new aspects of his inner world, and returns home changed, with new gifts and powers to share with his people. We see this same archetypal journey in Dante's passage through hell in the *Commedia*, Persephone's abduction into the underworld, and Saint John of the Cross's 'dark night of the soul', where painful experiences form the path to spiritual maturity.

One of our oldest myths teaches of a similar underworld journey into power and maturity. *The Descent of Inanna* is a Sumerian myth that has been carefully passed down to us on clay tablets that date back approximately six thousand years – perhaps an indication of its wisdom and value. The story tells how Inanna, Queen of the Great Above, ventures down into the underworld (the Great Below) to encounter her dark sister Ereshkigal. There in the underworld, she is killed and her body hung on a hook for three days and three nights, until the flesh is green and rotten. Eventually, helpers are sent from above – tiny figures carved out of dirt from under the god's fingernails. Offering empathy and compassion to Ereshkigal, these helpers secure Inanna's release. Fed with nectar from the gods, Inanna is brought back to life and returns to the Great Above to resume her role as Queen filled with new wisdom, power and insight from her journey through the dark.

In their different ways, these stories all point towards a leader's path through the 'underworld': a metaphor for our unconscious, the dark inner realm where unknown and forgotten parts of our soul reside. These forgotten qualities are what Carl Jung calls shadow. 'Shadow' does not mean they are dark or evil; sometimes our shadow includes golden qualities like ease, playfulness, joy, empowerment, spontaneity, compassion and intimacy. They are dark only in the sense that they are obscured from view, parts of our inner world that have been disowned by our conscious personality (the *ego*). To grow into our full power and leadership, we must descend into the unconscious and encounter our shadow – our 'dark sister'. In this encounter, old identities are destroyed and old patterns shed. Finally, through an act of grace, we return to the outer world whole: with new power, new wisdom and a new approach to leadership. Through this journey, we discover our essence: the full, pure expression of our selves – what I call *soul*.

In the light of these myths, it is perhaps not so surprising that contemporary journeys of transformation take us into forgotten, shadow aspects of life and leadership. Like Inanna or Campbell's archetypal hero, we too have to venture into the wilderness of our unconscious and discover little-known parts of our selves to find new sources of creativity, power and wisdom. In our journey of transformation, we too may have to let our lives 'hang on a hook' in the underworld for weeks, months or even years. Although this is frightening and uncomfortable, it eventually brings us to new skills, new insight, new perspectives and new ways of being in the world.

As we approach the mysteries of our shadow, it's important to remember that it's never a question of either–or. There's nothing wrong with the familiar mainstays of leadership: growth, activity, logic, conforming, strength and control. These are still important qualities for success.

However, at some stage, we simply can't grow any more by being more powerful, more busy, more factual, more adaptable, more resilient or more directional – and neither can our organizations and societies. To keep growing into our selves and into life, we have to open to new internal terrain: to dive into unknown and forgotten parts of our selves, and follow less-travelled paths to power, growth and success.

To venture into the 'underworld' of our unconscious is a frightening task, and it requires great courage. It's not easy to leave behind familiar identities, habits and attitudes and step into dark, unknown places in our inner and outer worlds. Nor is it easy to answer the questions that inevitably arise when we venture off the path and into the wilderness of soul; questions that we asked naturally as children, and learned to ignore with increasing determination as adults; questions that take courage to ask and to answer.

Who am I? What are my gifts? Am I using these gifts in my leadership, life and work? Does the organization I work for share my values? Am I co-creating a world that I am proud of? Or do I (or we, as an organization or community) need to change, to really move towards a compelling, sustainable and life-giving vision for the future?

Living these questions takes us on a journey of transformation, into courageous leadership. It's not an easy journey, but the rewards are immense. As we venture through the shadows of our unconscious, we come deeper into our selves. We make contact with our essence and we allow it to re-express itself in new and creative ways. We discover a new center of gravity: our inner truth, our authentic and wild self – our soul. Realigning our life and work around our wild self, we come 'home' to ourselves – and we find renewed passion, purpose and meaning in our leadership, life and work.

Reclaiming our shadow not only brings personal reward, it also helps us to support transformation in our teams, organizations, communities – and beyond. After all, it's not just personal crisis we face right now. Whole organizations, industries, communities, political systems, healthcare systems, financial systems and ecosystems are currently in crisis. Banks and established institutions are crumbling. Traditional political systems are unravelling. Economies teeter on the brink of collapse, weighed down by years of living beyond our means and 12-digit dollar deficits. The environment creaks under the strain of our demands: food shortages, pollution, water shortages and mass extinction whereby one in five species may die out by 2028.[1] Petroleum, central to so many aspects of human civilization, is in finite supply. A million people commit suicide every year, 60 per cent more than in 1955.[2] Ten per cent of people in the UK and 7 per cent of people in the USA are depressed.[3] Kids kill each other. These are not isolated crises. They are the symptoms of a wider change, of a deeper transformation. An old era is dissolving and a new era taking form, and like any process of change, this transition brings an element of chaos and destruction.

How can we support this change? What is our role, as leaders, in this wider journey of transformation?

Engaging in a personal journey of transformation is perhaps our most powerful way of supporting these wider changes. As Albert Einstein said, 'We cannot solve the problem with the consciousness that created the problem. We must learn to see the world anew.' When we integrate our shadow, we do indeed see the world anew. With our fresh eyes, we find new insight, new innovation and radically creative solutions to the challenges of our time. Ripples of our own personal journeys reach out across politics, education, business, the environment, healthcare and every other human system, paving the way for a vibrant and sustainable future. These changes begin in the inner world of each leader. They begin with you.

Engaging Your Journey

This book is for anyone ready to engage in a personal journey of transformation. Any number of things could be triggering that journey. Maybe you're facing obvious change in your working world – reorganization, redundancy, promotion, retirement, a move to a new company or industry – and want to consciously navigate those changes. Or maybe the call to change is more subtle – a longing for something more, a sense that you're not fulfilling your potential, a lack of purpose and meaning, the unshake-able sense that the 'real you' has got lost somewhere along your career path.

Regardless of your starting point, the intention of this book is to support you through your personal journey of transformation.

The next six chapters take you through the six thresholds of change. Each chapter explores one of these thresholds, guiding you on your inner journey through the shadows of Dying, Stillness, Intuition, Wildness, Vulnerability and Surrender.

All chapters follow a similar format. We begin with a story from my own journey of transformation, to start to bring this shadow quality to life. We then move into a more expansive conversation about this quality, exploring it from different perspectives, theories and traditions to see its nature, how it shows up in the shadow (and why), and what gifts it can offer us when we reclaim it. Finally, we turn to stories from inspirational and visionary leaders, sharing their experience with this shadow aspect of leadership and how it showed up in their journey of transformation.

Between chapters, I share practices to help you connect with the creativity and wisdom of your unconscious. These are intended to help you start to engage more actively in your own journey of change. You may find that the questions and changes you're working with are too big to engage alone, and that you need the support of an event, group or coach to fully engage with them in a way that feels safe and productive. Or you may feel ready to start to explore and open up these questions alone. If so, these practices can support you with that. Although loosely linked to the topic of the previous chapter, each practice stands alone as a gateway into the unconscious. So feel free to mix and match, and use whatever practice resonates for you. Some you may find easy and rich, others won't resonate at all. Go with what works for you.

Follow your own wisdom in how deeply to engage the practices and the themes of each chapter. You may find that just reading the book is enough for you. Or you might like to spend one week exploring each quality and deepening into the questions each chapter raises. Or if you're drawn to an even deeper exploration, you could give yourself one month for each quality, working through the book slowly over six months. You may well find, as I did while writing it, that life will bring its own initiations into each of the qualities, some more comfortable than others. Stay open to being surprised.

This is not a conventional business book. Yes, its stories and examples are anchored in the work world. Yet it's a book that is speaking to you, not your job title, and the scope of the conversation extends beyond the boundaries of the working world. As the stories show, we can encounter our shadow in any area of life: through our relationship with our boss or our relationship with our child or partner; through redundancy or divorce; through career challenges or personal challenges. Regardless of where we meet our shadow, the ripples of that encounter are felt throughout our lives – at home, at work and everywhere in between. Crises in any area of life can trigger, or dovetail with, journeys of transformation in our work life. So although the intention of this book is to challenge your view of leadership and the way you show up at work, the stories that highlight these changes include every aspect of life and living.

As you read these words, you might be experiencing the first stirrings of discontent, edging towards the precipice of change, descending into your shadow, suspended between your old approach to leadership and something new, lost in the darkness or slowly beginning to emerge. Wherever you are, may you find what you need in these pages. May the stories give you courage and inspiration to follow the call of your soul, wherever it may lead. May the path through the shadows be rich and rewarding. And may all our journeys carry us safely into a new and sustainable world.

CHAPTER 1

Dying

Making Space for Change

The important thing is this: to be able at any moment
to sacrifice what we are for what we could become.

– CHARLES DUBOIS –

How can we step towards the future
if we don't let go of the past?

And how can we grow into the leader we are becoming
if we don't find the courage
to die to the leader we have been?

Making Friends with Dying: My Story

The unravelling of my life came unannounced. I was 24, living and working in Thailand as a brand manager for Sunsilk, Unilever's largest hair-care brand. It was a glamorous and exciting time of my life. I lived in a beautiful 18th-floor apartment, with three bedrooms, wooden floors, stylish Asian furniture and a balcony that looked out across the glittering lights of Bangkok. Every morning, Lek, my driver, waited patiently outside my home to pick me up and weave his way gracefully through beeping horns, tuk-tuks and often-flooded streets, delivering me in air-conditioned comfort to the office. At home, someone else cooked, cleaned, shopped and did my laundry for me. It was a life of luxury beyond my imaginings.

Meanwhile, I was on the fast track to career glory – or so I thought. I was leading a hugely exciting innovation project: a new type of hair colourant, which our market research suggested would revolutionize the market and create €100 million of incremental turnover every year. Reporting directly to the brand director, I had an enviable amount of freedom, responsibility and exposure to senior people in Unilever. I flew around Asia visiting women in cities and far-flung rural villages – and was paid for the privilege!

We were one month away from launch, with the product made, packed and ready to ship. It was a regular Friday afternoon in the overly-air-conditioned Bangkok office, and my boss and I were heading out the door to the advertising agency to finalize the details of our launch campaign. Laptops over our shoulders, we were almost out the door when the technical director stopped us and beckoned us into his office. 'I'm afraid we've got some bad news,' he said. 'We just got the results of the long-term usage tests. There may be a problem with the product. We're going to have to cancel the launch.' Just like that, the project I had poured my heart, mind and soul into for the last 18 months vanished.

An hour later, I sat with my project team in a gloomy, soulless bar, staring at my beer in stunned silence. Behind the initial shock, I could feel the first signs of a deep disappointment settling heavy and grey on my heart. Behind that, something even more unsettling: a profound kind of disorientation. My boss and his boss had already reassured me that there would be another project for me in Bangkok. So the loss of direction was not a literal fear of losing my job, but a more subtle, internal disorientation. The bank-holiday weekend yawned ahead of me, a grey nothingness. And beyond it – what? What was my life anchored to, if not this project? What did I care about, beyond its success and mine? Why was I here, in this strange country, so far from friends and family? Where was I going? Who had I become?

That evening, in a foggy, depressed state, I dug out a piece of paper I'd been given months before and booked a massage at the (aptly named) New Beginnings healing centre. Three days later, on my 25th birthday, I set out across a congested bank-holiday Bangkok feeling lost, alone and miserable. It was humid and sticky, and as I walked down the dusty side street that housed New Beginnings, there was a faint smell of sewage. Feral dogs lay at the side of the road, watching warily as I walked past. New Beginnings was at the end of the road; emotionally, so was I.

What happened in the next few hours shook up my view of the world as a rational place. Technically I had a shiatsu massage, with a bit of 'energy healing' at the end. I'd never heard of energy healing, and as far as I could tell it seemed to involve the therapist holding his hands a few inches away from my body and doing ... well, nothing. But it felt good, deeply relaxing. Afterwards, as I walked out of New Beginnings, I felt radiant. I didn't care about the smell of sewage. I wasn't afraid of the feral dogs. The grayness of only hours before had turned into a tingling sense of vitality and possibility. I could feel life pulsing inside me, and I was ready to live it.

Although I didn't know it at the time, these strange and new encounters with my soul heralded the death of my old life and old identities. Over the next six months, I went every weekend to New Beginnings. There, I practised meditation, learned about energy systems of the body, qualified as a Reiki practitioner, had my first tarot reading. Despite my initial scepticism, these experiences began to change me. I softened. I became less aggressive and less driven; more patient, more compassionate, more gentle. Gradually, the old masks of 'independent, ambitious, competitive high achiever' began to fall away, and someone new started to emerge from within.

It took time for the inner changes to filter into my outer world. I stayed with Unilever for 18 months, accepting promotion to a global role in Argentina. I still lived in beautiful homes and flew around the world business class – and I enjoyed that lifestyle. But I began to separate my identity from these outer achievements and conventional indicators of 'success'. As I continued to explore my inner world through therapy, dream work, energy healing, shamanism, meditation, creative visualization, yoga and other spiritual practices, the longings of my heart began slowly to reveal themselves to me.

So it was that, 18 months after the unravelling began, I found myself in another soulless bar, this time inside a five-star hotel in Buenos Aires with the senior vice president of Unilever's hair category. He was my boss's boss's boss, layers of management above me, smart, successful and (sometimes painfully) honest. I admired him. 'I don't get involved in many people's careers,' he said, 'but I want to support you. Where would you like to go? America? Europe? Whatever you want, we can make it happen.'

For a moment, my career path glittered ahead of me. I felt the generosity of his offer, and I felt its seduction. I wanted to impress and to please. I wanted to be 'successful' and to enjoy the glamour of international life. I wanted a monthly paycheck, the security of a pension, the promise of paid maternity leave at some point in the future. But more than all those things, I wanted to come alive. And I knew, from what I'd learned about myself over the last 18 months, that I could not do that in the corporate world. I could grow there, yes. But I would grow like a tree on the side of a wind-swept mountain: twisted, out of balance, rough. I could grow mentally, professionally, financially. I might grow tall, my roots clinging tightly to their rocky foundation. But I would never blossom there.

So I looked back at this man sitting across from me in that corporate bar, swallowed my fear and turned into Dying. 'I think I'm going to take an unpaid sabbatical,' I told him. A few weeks later, I left Unilever and headed fiercely into the unknown.

The Nature of Dying

Just when the caterpillar thought the world
was over, it became a butterfly.

– ANONYMOUS

While we humans twist ourselves into knots resisting endings and the 'little deaths' in our lives, the natural world models change with elegance and grace. Every day trees, animals, ocean, sun, moon and stars tirelessly enter into the natural movement of life, following its inevitable journey through death into rebirth. In our turning world, the sun can only appear over the horizon because it set the night before. Trees can only bud and sprout new leaves because they shed the dying leaves the previous fall. The tide can only rise because it fell. The moon can only wax because it waned. We can only breathe in because we breathe out. New cells can only grow because old cells die. Over and over again, we see that the natural order of things is to shed what is dying to make space for new life.

The caterpillar offers us a particularly vivid example of this. Ferociously munching its way through leaves and plants, a caterpillar sheds its skin four or five times as it grows. Each time, it wriggles out of its old skin and reveals a fresh, identical skin underneath. That works for a while, but then something mysterious happens. At some point, a biological mechanism in the caterpillar detects that its skin has stretched as far as it will go. It can't simply shed this skin and form another one. Something in the caterpillar knows that it's reached the end of the road. That its time as a caterpillar has come to an end. That the old strategies have got it as far as they can, and that it's now time for a more fundamental change. So the caterpillar stops feeding and begins wandering in search of a suitable place to transform into its next form: *a pupa*. When it finds this place it stops and molts its skin one last time. It becomes a cocoon or chrysalis. And so it enters the next stage of its life.

As the cocoon, the pupa neither moves nor feeds. It withdraws into a silent, still place where it is not actively engaged with the outside world. Here, the larval structures are broken down and the adult structures begin to take form. While this happens, it is betwixt and between. It is in some kind of liminal place where it is neither caterpillar nor butterfly.

Finally, by some mysterious process, the pupa emerges from the cocoon as a butterfly. It rests on the surface of its cocoon, waiting for its wings to dry. Then it opens its colourful wings and takes flight. Its transformation is complete. In this beautiful butterfly, the DNA of the caterpillar is still there. It's the same creature with the same essence. Yet it's taken on a radically new form.

The journey of the caterpillar suggests two levels of Dying. The first is a shedding of skins: wriggling out of old, dying skins to reveal similar skins that have been forming underneath. In the human world, shedding our skins might mean letting go of one job, and moving up to the next layer of management in the same organization or industry. It might mean terminating one product variant, project or client relationship and replacing it with a new one that is superficially different yet fundamentally the same. It might mean wriggling out of one five-year plan and into another, virtually identical strategy. It might mean tweaking political policies, within an established and traditional framework. All these changes are little deaths, helping us stay current and alive within consistent, familiar contexts, traditions and identities.

Over time, these surface layers of shedding lead us towards the second level of Dying: a more radical change where our identity, habits, perspectives and needs are fundamentally re-invented, renewed and re-forged from the inside out. This deeper transformation requires a three-stage process. First, we leave behind the caterpillar – our familiar habits, identities, perspectives and traditions. Second, we enter the chrysalis, opening to a disorientating time in between our old reality and something new. Finally, we emerge as a butterfly, with a wholly new identity, form and way of being in the world.

Human beings across time have engaged similar three-stage models of transformative change. In his 1909 publication *Les Rites de Passage*, French ethnographist and anthropologist Arnold van Gennep presents one such map. Studying traditions from cultures across the world, van Gennep looked at how humans ceremonially engage with moments of transition – whether that transition is setting out on a journey, entering a temple or moving from one life stage to the next. He suggested that there are consistently three phases in these ceremonies. First, cut from what we know; second, enter a liminal time, where we are between worlds; third, re-enter everyday life, bringing insights and gifts from the ceremony with us. Van Gennep called these three phases Severance, Threshold and Incorporation.

Later, van Gennep's work became the foundation for other models of change. In 1949, when American mythologist Joseph Campbell wrote about the Hero's Journey, he described similar phases: Departure, Initiation and Return. In 1979, William Bridges's writings on transitions also mapped out three phases: Endings, Thresholds and New Beginnings. Whether we lean on the natural model of caterpillar to butterfly or on these human models of change, the journey is the same: a process of Dying that brings us across a Threshold and finally out into a new world.

The Journey of Change

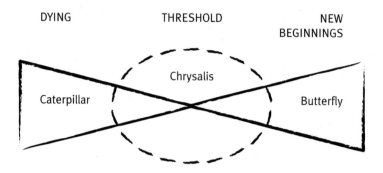

DYING THRESHOLD NEW BEGINNINGS

Caterpillar Chrysalis Butterfly

Dying usually shows up as some kind of disruption. Often the disruption can be quite subtle – irritation, impatience, insomnia, dissatisfaction with our current situation, and/or a deep longing for something new or different. Other times, especially if we fail to listen to the inner signs, the call for change can be louder and more dramatic – outer events like illness, depression, redundancy, economic decline or a changing market. When we open to this disruption, we enter into the process of Dying, allowing our old world to dissolve and fall away both internally and externally – beliefs, attitudes, perspectives, relationships, habits, forms, structures and systems. This Dying leads us into the centre of the transformation: the Threshold, an in-between space, where the old world has fallen away and the new world has not yet formed. Here, our attention turns towards an inner transformation. Listening deeply to what is stirring within us, we lean towards what waits to be born, what calls to us from beyond the Threshold. As we give our attention to the new life that is emerging from within us, we are drawn forward into New Beginnings. Here, we reap the rewards of the journey and step back out into the world in new identities, perspectives, beliefs and possibilities.

The entire transformational process is a funnel. When Dying first breaks in, our life is full, diverse and complex. For a time, we engage with Dying on a surface level, shedding our skins and wriggling into new ones. After a time, though, we realize that our skins have become too tight, too small, too narrow. As we accept this, we turn inside, leaning our awareness into our core and consciously engaging a process of radical simplification, so that we arrive at the Threshold small enough to pass through the eye of the needle. Stripped bare, we enter the Threshold: a time of emptiness, of introspection, of staying close to home – a time in our cocoon. Finally, after some time suspended in this in-between place, we venture out into the world again, evolving and emerging, slowly at first, and then with more confidence and conviction. So the funnel broadens out again, and our lives grow and expand into new territories and experiences.

It's important to note that this process is not linear. We are pulled to the edge of the dying process again and again. Each time we think: *Surely this is it? Surely this is the last layer of letting go? Surely the new life will come in now?* And indeed, a piece of our new life might well come in. Then a few months later, we have to let something else go – a friend, a lover, a belief, a dream. And so round and round we go between Dying, the emptiness of the Threshold, New Beginnings. Our emerging reality can never be held on to. At some point, we grow out of each new, bigger world, and we have to dive into the journey of change all over again. We never arrive – or, rather, we arrive only into the present moment. In every moment, we are simultaneously becoming something and leaving something else behind. There is no solid ground. Death and rebirth is a timeless cycle with no end and no beginning. Knowing this, can we turn into change over and over, again and again, following its path through Dying into new life?

Reclaiming Dying

Man cannot discover new oceans
unless he has the courage to lose sight of the shore.

– ANDRÉ GIDE

Does the caterpillar cry, shout and throw a tantrum when he senses he has shed his skin for the last time and reached the end of the caterpillar road? Maybe he does in his own way. But no matter how much he mourns the end of his existence as a caterpillar, it does not change things. His time is up. His skin has stretched enough times and has no more room to grow. So the caterpillar must let go of his identity as caterpillar. He must find the courage to withdraw from life, enter his cocoon and allow himself to transform into a butterfly. He must willingly embrace the process of death and rebirth. Unfortunately, he cannot be butterfly and caterpillar at the same time. That's just the way it is.

The same is true in the human world. Here, even small changes can trigger a low level of fear and anxiety – changing roles, moving office, de-listing a variant, withdrawing funding from a particular project or client. So we stay in a familiar team even though we have become bored with the job; we continue to produce old variants and add the new ones incrementally; we increase spending to fund old *and* new projects and clients; we refuse to make sacrifices – and hold on to our old skins long after we should have shed them.

When it comes to deeper transformation, our fear is magnified. Entering into the narrowing funnel, we are asked to let go of the traditions, structures, habits, beliefs, identities and perspectives of the past and open to something fundamentally different. That might mean downsizing our home to pursue a radically different career path. It might mean closing a factory and radically re-inventing production strategy for a new world. It might mean withdrawing a brand from the market to focus on emerging markets, or closing down an arm of the business to focus on a different set of clients. It might mean withdrawing investment in a dying industry (coal, typewriters, VHS, CDs) to prioritize new technologies.

Often, we are asked to engage in the Dying before the new world has begun to emerge. We are asked to let go of who we have been, without knowing who we will become – to step into the hollowed-out, in-between emptiness of the Threshold, with its eerie, disorientating stillness. Here, we may feel that nothing is happening. We may feel lost, unsure of what direction to take. We may feel bored or frustrated, longing for change and new life that is not yet here. Our days may feel empty, our goals hazy and our lives directionless. Sometimes we are suspended in this Threshold for weeks, sometimes months, sometimes years. Although we desperately want to move into action, we don't yet know what action to take. Often, we wonder whether new life will appear at all on the other side of this process of transformation. Driven by these fears, we may be tempted to fall back into the known and try to resuscitate our fading reality, or to skip ahead and reach for a new world without fully unravelling and releasing the old. Giving in to these fears we short-circuit the cycles of change and miss the deeper opportunities within them.

Our tendency to avoid Dying holds true at many levels, from the individual to the global. As leaders, we try to enter new territories with the tools that generated success for us in our old world. So if efficiency has been one of our strengths, we may try to do more, more quickly. If decisiveness is our strength, we may continue to make quick decisions (even as those decisions become more complex and less clear in a changing world). Other times, we superficially engage with Dying but refuse to make the deeper, internal changes. Letting go is not just about quitting a job; it's about consciously shedding the identities that we attached to that job. It's not just about accepting market decline; it's about leaving behind the beliefs, habits and ways of being in the world that are leading to that decline.

When we hear the call for deeper change, we have a choice. We can resist it and struggle on with old habits, beliefs, traditions and perspectives. Or we can turn into the journey of transformation and follow it through to a new reality. Facing redundancy, do we simply reach for the next available job – or do we turn inwards and use the crisis as an opportunity to review our life, our goals, our deeper longings and the kind of work we really want to do? Recovering from illness, do we push the experience away and insist on getting on with our lives; or do we turn into the journey of change and rethink our whole approach to life? Standing on the precipice of a crumbling financial reality, do we simply pour more money into the old systems – or do we courageously reinvent our selves and our systems for our emerging world? Do we shed our skins or do we enter into the transformational journey?

Sometimes whole industries face this choice. In today's world, the publishing and music industries are good examples. Both are sitting with challenging questions: *What's our place in this changing world, where people can download books and music instantly, sometimes for free?* Similarly, the airline industry is asking: *How do we make money in a world where people now expect to fly for less money than it costs to drive or take the train – and a world where, simultaneously, fuel prices and taxes are rising?* The advertising industry is confronting the question: *How do we communicate with this new, digitally connected human being (who, incidentally, can now use TiVo or Sky+ to skip through advertising campaigns that companies have paid millions of pounds for)?* Shedding their skin is not going to carry these industries successfully and profitably into our emerging future. They need to transform more radically – just as Wilkinson Sword did a hundred years ago, when its market for swords began to decline and it was forced to reinvent itself by transforming its expertise in blades into new markets: razor blades and garden tools.

Even entire societies and economies face a similar choice right now. Do we bail out our banks and failing financial institutions, propping up the dying economic systems they represent? Or do we engage with the deeper changes of our time and ask ourselves more fundamental, frightening questions? Questions like: *Is it sustainable to build a society on debt? What are the risks and consequences, for people and planet? Do our current financial systems really serve the bigger picture? Is it time to dismantle the assumptions and structures that our economies have been built on and make space for a new understanding of money and value?* To engage with these questions, we risk dying to what we have known, in order to find fundamentally new ways of being in the world.

When we do find the courage to turn into a deeper transformation, we are showered with its gifts: new life, new energy and new possibilities. Emerging from the cocoon, we may step into new levels of responsibility or embark on wholly new careers. Or perhaps we recommit to our previous job, yet bring our new self into it so that the way we do our work is different – we're freer, more empowered, more joyful, more alive. Organizations return to growth after a period of decline or stagnation, revitalized by new perspectives, new beliefs and new expressions of their values. Our sense of identity expands, and with it our outer world also begins to get bigger. Metaphorically, we are reborn.

Apple's CEO Steve Jobs is an inspiring example of a leader who engaged Dying in this more radical way. Having started the company in his parents' garage in 1976, at the age of 30 Jobs had already reached the pinnacle of success. In 1985 Apple was a $2 billion business with 4,000 employees. It had also just released what Jobs calls 'its finest creation' – the Macintosh. Then came the disruption – Jobs got fired from his own company! In a falling-out between Jobs and the newly appointed CEO, the Board of Directors sided with the CEO, and Jobs was out. What had been the focus of his whole adult life was now gone. And, as he told graduating students at Stanford University, he was devastated.

Ultimately, though, Jobs' encounter with Dying made possible his famous success. Although he didn't see it that way at the time, Jobs now describes getting fired from Apple as the best thing that could have ever happened to him. Free to be a beginner again, he entered one of the most creative periods of his life. During the next five years, Jobs started two new companies, NeXT and Pixar, and fell in love with his wife. Pixar went on to create the world's first computer-animated feature film, *Toy Story*, and is now a highly successful animation studio. Meanwhile, in an unexpected turn of events, Apple bought NeXT and Jobs returned to Apple. The technology developed at NeXT formed an important part of Apple's current renaissance. So his unexpected and unwanted encounter with Dying led Jobs into new opportunities, prosperity and happiness. As he acknowledges, most likely none of this would have happened if he hadn't been fired from Apple.[4]

To face Dying can be frightening. Yet ultimately, being willing to die to the past (and to who we have been in the past) is the only way to stay truly alive in a world that demands both life and death. If we don't let go of the past, we cannot find our way into the future. If we don't let go of who we have been, we cannot discover who we are becoming. Without Dying, life cannot sustain itself. As Goethe says, in 'The Holy Longing':

> So long as you have not experienced this,
> to die and so to grow,
> you are merely a troubled guest on this earth.[5]

The Journey into Dying

What we call the beginning is often the end
And to make an end is to make a beginning.
The end is where we start from.

– T S ELIOT

In the modern, Western world, death is held safely out of view. Walled off from the natural world, living in concrete societies that override the rhythms of life, we have lost touch with Dying. This was not always the case. Our ancestors lived much closer to death. People killed their own food, women died in childbirth, illness spread through the village with no drugs to keep it at bay. The awareness of mortality was close at hand. Because death was a part of our ancestors' reality, it was also a part of their psyche. They understood how to approach and engage Dying, in both its physical and its psychological forms.

So, as we turn towards change, we may find it useful to examine the myths, traditions and ceremonies of our ancestors, and to borrow their insight into how to engage with dying and rebirth. One of these traditions is the ancient Mayan ceremony of the Great Ballcourt.[6] The remains of ballcourts are found among the ruins of temple complexes across Mexico and South America, and can be traced back to around 1500 to 800 BC. The exact nature of the game is not known. We do know that it involved stone rings and rubber balls, and experts suggest a game something along the lines of modern-day basketball. From the ballcourt panels, we also know that the game sometimes included ritual sacrifice – not, as we might imagine, of the loser, but, according to Joseph Campbell, of the captain of the *winning* team.

In the Mayan world, playing on the Great Ballcourt risked a literal death. To prepare, potential players went through a series of steps. First came Decision Road. Here, those who had been invited to play had to decide whether they were willing to risk everything and participate in the game.

Once the player had decided to step onto Decision Road, he began a psychological preparation for what lay ahead. The Mayans understood that to be able to play freely on the Ballcourt, the player needed to have attended to all unfinished business. He could not afford to be distracted in the critical moment by regrets, unresolved feelings or things left unsaid. And so they created a Death Lodge and invited people to come and visit them there, to make good their social relationships. In the Death Lodge, the player asked for forgiveness, gave forgiveness, expressed his gratitude for the life he had lived so far and shared his love with the people who had made it meaningful. The player spent several days in the Death Lodge, saying goodbye and preparing for his possible death. Finally, the night before the game, he entered the third stage of preparation: the Purpose Circle. This was an all-night vigil, spent alone on the edge of a pit filled with the skulls of previous Ballcourt winners – literally looking death in the face. In the Death Lodge the player made good his relationships with others, in the Purpose Circle he made good his relationship with himself. *What have I achieved? What has my life been about? What am I proud of? What do I regret? Has it been enough?* Through these questions, the player made peace with himself and his life, with all its beauty and failings. Only then could he surrender fully into the game the next day. Stepping onto the Great Ballcourt, he entered the Threshold between life and death, and played for his life.

For the Mayans, the sacrifice of the winning player was not just a gory, meaningless death. It was a ritual enactment of death and rebirth. When the game was over, news spread across the community. Fires, lamps and torches were put out until the whole land was in darkness. In darkness, the player was sacrificed. As he died, a torch was lit, and that torch was used to light other torches, until light spread through the community once more. In this way, the Mayan people acknowledged the sacrifice of the Ballcourt player and the regeneration that his death made possible for the community. Acting out this regeneration in such a dramatic way kept the understanding of dying and rebirth alive.

It's easy to get caught in the horror of a ceremony that centres around human sacrifice. It's simply not something we understand in the modern world. For us, it's barbaric, inhumane, crazy. But if we move behind the literal events of the ceremony, we can access its symbolic meaning. And from that meaning, we can borrow insight and understanding into the little deaths that we experience throughout our lives; we can become familiar with the nature of psychological death and rebirth.

The four stages that the Ballcourt player went through are equally relevant to each of us when we find ourselves on the threshold of change. We can follow this process when we leave a job, when we face retirement, when we prepare for divorce, when we are challenged with illness, when we find our business or market in decline, or when we simply feel the longing for something different, something more, in our work and life. The four stages are:

1. Decision Road: Will I step into the journey of change? Can I find the courage to acknowledge 'I'm dying' / 'something in my life is dying' / 'my old ways of living and working are dying'? Can I willingly walk into my possible death, just like the Ballcourt player?

2. Death Lodge: What do I need to say or do to bring my relationships current? Who do I need to forgive? Who do I need to ask for forgiveness? Is there anything left unsaid in my work or personal relationships? Am I ready to say goodbye?

3. Purpose Circle: What have I learned and who have I become in this stage of my life? What am I proud of? What do I regret? What needs to happen for me to make peace with myself? Can I find meaning in the challenges, difficulties and disappointments I've encountered? What have I not yet lived?

4. The Great Ballcourt: Can I step into the Threshold and open fully to an unknown future? What new world is emerging in the emptiness? What gifts and resources can I access to help me through this moment? What new gifts do I discover in it?

To engage in these four steps is to engage with Dying itself. Just as importantly, it opens us to life. As we compassionately release the past, with all its joys and sorrows, we step into the emptiness of the Threshold. Shedding the old stories, wounds, habits, beliefs and identities, we make space for something new to emerge. Courageously turning into Dying, we are showered with new life.

Dying and the Birth of Method

Eric Ryan, Founder, Method Inc

Method is a US-based organization launched in 2001 by Eric Ryan and Adam Lowry. They offer a range of cleaning products that are brightly coloured, stylishly packaged and environmentally advanced: chemical-free, working without the toxic ingredients of conventional cleaning products. This innovative approach has created value in a traditionally dull category, allowing Method to charge two to three times more than their competitors, and has led to strong financial success: Method was ranked as the seventh-fastest-growing company in the USA by Ink magazine in 2006, and was number 16 on Fast Company's list of Most Innovative Companies; in 2008, its turnover was $100 million. Yet like all new beginnings, that success came through a challenging journey of sacrifices and endings.

Ever since he was a child, Eric had wanted to be an entrepreneur. In the third grade, he sold buttons door to door; at middle school, he opened a bookstore. Yet, as he hit his late 20s, his dreams of creating his own business were still just that: dreams. Meanwhile, he was working in advertising, earning more and more money, and easing into a comfortable, safe life.

Then came the disruption. 'There were two jarring moments that got me to say: "Okay, now's the time to do it." I had a boss who was horrible to work for, and I swore I would never work for anyone again. Then, my girlfriend at the time (who's now my wife!) broke up with me for someone else. With those two moments colliding, I was pretty miserable for the first time in my life, and I found myself thinking: "Now's the time to create change."'

Even before these moments of disruption, Eric had been playing with business ideas and working them up in a notebook. Yet until disruption hit, he had never made it across the first threshold of commitment: telling someone else about his plan! 'I was embarrassed to talk about it, at the beginning, particularly because cleaning products is not a cool industry by any means.' As he studied the markets, Eric had bought a lot of products, but they were stashed out of sight under his bed.

Finally, though, on a ski trip with his roommate (and co-founder) Adam, Eric finally confessed what he was doing and shared his dream of creating Method. 'Saying the idea out loud was a really difficult process – partly because it made it real and put me on a hook; partly because I was embarrassed to be seen to take it on. So simply coming out of the closet was the first threshold.'

Meeting a positive response from Adam, Eric took another step towards launch: creating a Concept Book that brought to life the key elements of the idea and business plan. He gave this book to 20 people from different walks of life, whose opinion he respected, and said to them, 'Tell me why this is going to fail.' The best any of them could offer was: 'If it's so right, why has no-one done it before?' With this outer validation, the pull towards launching Method became stronger.

To fully claim this opportunity, Eric and Adam had to die to their old realities. For Eric, that began with quitting his job in advertising and working freelance, so that he would have more time to develop Method. This worked for some time, but eventually it came to crunch-point: committing fully to Method and walking away from even his freelance work. 'It was the dot-com explosion, and money was oozing through the streets of San Francisco with start-ups who needed marketing help. I realized that I was going to have to just go cold turkey on it.' So he walked away from the prestige, identity, income and structure of freelance work and took one step further towards his dream. Then came the next step. Eric took $50,000 he had inherited from his grandfather and invested it in the business; Adam invested another $50,000. That was scary, but the final step was even scarier: asking friends and family to take a leap of faith and invest in Method. As Eric says, 'Taking their hard-earned money felt like a huge amount of pressure – now we really had to make it work!'

The path to success was filled with moments of doubt – and still is. There were many times when the founders wondered if they were going to make it into the small percentages of start-up companies that actually become sustainable businesses. As Eric said: 'We knew what failure would look like – it looked like folding the business, facing the embarrassment of telling people it hadn't worked out (and worse still, telling our investors that they wouldn't be getting their money back), and going to business school. But we didn't want that to happen. And at each stage, as we committed more to the business, it became harder to go back than to go forwards.' Slowly, then, the founders of Method shifted their energy from their old reality and moved through the threshold of change into a new beginning. That beginning could never have happened without a willingness to die to the old way – externally and internally.

As Method evolves and matures, Dying and growing still continue to weave themselves together. At an organizational level, that means restructuring the organization to keep up with rapid growth. Often that has meant hiring in new people over the top of existing employees, so that Method can keep growing into its full potential. In 2009, Method changed half their leadership team. As Eric says, 'People are used to working in companies where their skills grow faster than the company. In a start-up like Method, the company grows faster than the people. That can be difficult for people to take, and it means we've had to let go of a lot of employees.'

Dying has also continued to make itself felt at a personal level in Eric's leadership style. As the business has matured, Eric's role has changed. 'Launching the business needed huge amounts of will, vision and drive – a bit like the energy you need to launch a rocket. Yet, to scale the business, that level of drive and control wasn't possible or even helpful.' So he had to learn new skills, and redefine his role within the business. 'Having an idea and pushing it through to completion was no longer my role. My role became setting juicy, inspiring goals and helping people get behind them.' Accepting these changes involved sacrifice. When Method was small, Eric had complete control over how things happened. As it grew, he no longer had final say over pack design, copy, product placement or fragrance. To allow the business to grow and change, Eric had to mature and change as a leader.

Method's story shows how Dying weaves through every stage of launching, growing and running a business. In Eric's experience we see what's possible when we find the courage to let go and lean into new life as it emerges – over and over again.

Source: My interview with Eric Ryan

PRACTICE # 1

Journaling

When you want to access the wisdom of your unconscious, journaling is a great place to start. It works on the premise that some part of you already has the answers to the questions you're living. By journaling, you move around the part of you that's blocked or confused, and you open to hidden resources in the unconscious. And you can do it anywhere – even on your journey to or from work.

There are no rules in journaling, but here are some guidelines.

1. Begin with a clear **intention** – some area of your work or life that you'd like insight into. This could be one of the questions raised in this book, a challenge you're facing in your work, something as simple as *Where am I in my life right now?* or a more general intention to deepen your relationship with a certain quality. For example, to deepen your exploration of Dying, you might like to journal around the following statements:

    • In my life right now . . .
    • If I had no fear I would . . .
    • Deep down I know . . .
    • I'm ready to say goodbye to . . .
    • If anything were possible . . .

2. **Set the parameters.** Decide how long you are going to write for. As a rule, I'd suggest no less than 10 minutes, and no more than 30 minutes. You might prefer to set the limits around length rather than time – for example, writing three pages.

3. **Start writing . . . and do not stop!** This is probably the most

important part of the experience. The idea is to enter into something of a flow state, from which you can tap into your intuition, connecting to the right brain and its access to the unconscious. So keep writing, even if that means writing: *Hmmm . . . I seem to have run out of things to say about this. Well, I guess there might be something important to explore around this other idea . . .* Let your writing flow around any blocks you encounter. Don't judge what you write or try to make sense of it. Just write. Often, it helps to write in a question–answer format, letting each question deepen the exploration by drilling down from what you're discovering into the next layer of insight.

4. When the time is up, or you've reached the allocated number of pages, stop. **Close the experience**, walk away from what you've written, and intentionally step back into your everyday consciousness.

5. Come back to your words after a break or some time later that day. Re-read what you've written and **look for themes**, paying attention to patterns, words or images that recur. Notice anything that surprises you. Anything that stirs up a strong feeling – fear, excitement, longing, grief.

6. Is there any action or **commitment** you need to take, based on the insights from your writing experience? If so, take it.

CHAPTER 2

Stillness

Trusting the Emptiness

What a surprise to the caterpillar
when the call to be quiet,
contemplative and still
results in the ability to fly.

– NAVAJO –

And so – courageously shedding what's Dying,
we find ourselves in the Stillness of the Threshold.
Pause, reflection, disorientation, rest.
What might be possible if we trusted this emptiness?

Face to Face with Stillness: My Story

One of the scariest things about quitting Unilever was the sudden loss of structure. Until that point, my life had always had a timetable. As a student, that was lessons, homework, out-of-school activities and socializing. Later, it was the 9-to-5 day, with its schedule of meetings, activities and demands on my time. Now, however, I found myself facing an indefinite period of emptiness. My days had no structure and no goals. No one was telling me where to go or what to do. I was directionless, operating in a world without definition, boundaries or routine. It was disorientating, exhilarating and deeply unsettling.

Wanting to fill this space with something useful (and perhaps, unconsciously, wanting to tranquilize the rising panic within me), I signed up for a spiritual workshop with a man called Brugh Joy. In October 2004, two weeks after leaving Unilever, I flew from Buenos Aires to LA and headed into a one-week retreat in the desert of Lone Pine, California.

The first few days of that retreat were wonderful, nourishing and full. We shared our life stories, and Brugh offered insight and challenge to help us deepen those stories. We worked with dreams. We ate good food and spent time walking through the silent desert landscape. On day three of seven, things were ticking along nicely. I was even getting used to the 'No Cell Phone and No E-mail' rule. Everything was going well. Then Brugh made an announcement. 'We're going to have a day off tomorrow,' he told us. 'I'd like you to spend it alone, in silence and fasting. There'll be no sessions and no meals. I highly suggest you don't read or listen to music. I'll see you back here at 7am the day after tomorrow.'

This was an unexpected announcement. To the busy executive within me, it was also wholly unwelcome. Thirty-six hours with no activities, no talking and no food? I hadn't been warned of this when I signed up. Was I paying hundreds of dollars for *this*? What a ridiculous waste of time! Behind these objections lay a deeper emotion: terror. Thirty-six hours of emptiness.

What was I going to do with all that time? How would I fill my day? Would it feel like an eternity? How would I survive the boredom of it? Behind the boredom, what unwelcome insights and feelings might I discover?

I tried to swallow my rising panic as I sorted through my mental filing cabinet for a plan. My Western, goal-focused mind finally locked in on a solution. Brugh had mentioned something about an *ashrama* – a small stone hut on the mountainside. Perhaps hiking there would be a way to fill my long, empty day? Falling asleep that night, on the edge of emptiness, I comforted myself with the knowledge that I had a plan.

The next morning I headed up the mountainside in search of the ashrama. I had no map, and only a vague memory of how to get there: head up the mountain, turn right on the first trail and keep going. It sounded easy enough. Two hours later, I was at the same place, on the same trail, still heading up. I'd been up and down this same trail three times. Somehow I seemed to keep missing 'the first turning to the right'. Still, I was not to be defeated. I had a plan, and that plan was to make it to the ashrama. That's what I'd decided, and that is what I would do. Without that plan, I would have to face a much more uncomfortable proposition: doing nothing. And doing nothing was not something I did well.

It was starting to get pretty hot in the midday California sun, and I still hadn't located the first trail to the right. Instead, I found myself in a crop of shaggy rocks, looking out across the desert towards snow-capped mountains. Tired from the exertion of climbing up and down the trail, I negotiated a short rest. Leaning against the cool surface of the rock, I gazed out across the landscape. For the first time that day, I noticed its beauty. The sky was a vibrant blue and the mountains were all around me, holding me. The bare desert landscape shimmered in the sunlight. I longed to sit here and rest. To just *be*.

But then I looked around again, and this time I started to wonder. Were there wolves out here? Bears? No one knew where I was. Was it really safe to just sit here, out in the middle of the desert, alone? Anyway, what about the ashrama? I had set myself a task; I was not going to just give up. So with mild reluctance, I got up again and headed down the mountain in search of the path one more time. This time, inexplicably, I noticed a trail I hadn't seen before and tried it out.

A few minutes later, a wonderful sight came into view. A person was walking along the path towards me! As he got closer, I recognized him as Robert, one of the guys from our group. There followed a silent, somewhat comic interchange. 'Ashrama?' I mouthed, pointing at the trail he was returning along. He nodded. Relief. Finally, I was on the right path. I stretched my arms wide, then moved them closer together, with my head on one side and what I hoped was a quizzical look on my face. 'How far?' I was trying to say. He put up two fingers and nodded encouragingly. Two what? I wondered. Two miles? Two hours? Two minutes? I couldn't think of a way to ask that in sign language, so we smiled and parted. My legs were tiring, and I felt quietly jealous of Robert as he headed home. But it was still only 2pm and there were lots of hours to fill yet. So I carried on with my plan.

It was 3pm when I finally saw it: a stone hut nestled into the mountain-side. I had made it! Exhilarated and triumphant, I walked through the rotting wooden doorway and sat on the earth in the centre of the ashrama. The air was cool and damp, and there was a deep sense of silence. I walked around, visiting the four corners, and feeling into the energy of the place. *Perhaps I could do a ceremony here?* I wondered, half-heartedly. But I was distracted. It was late in the afternoon, and I was a long way from home with no flashlight. How far had I walked? How long was it going to take me to get home? What time did the sun set? How many hours until dark? I went through the motions of sitting quietly for a while and tried to find some sense of stillness and peace, but my anxious mind kept pulling me back. With all my worrying and planning, I just couldn't seem to settle into the stillness. I figured I might as well head home.

An hour later, I passed the spot where I'd met Robert earlier in the day. To my surprise, he was still there, sitting by the side of the road, leaning against a rock, watching the sun streak the sky pink. He looked calm, blissful even. I sat down next to him, and took in the spectacular sky and the spreading shadows that muted the sage and rocks. The silence felt calm and nourishing, and I was filled with a deep sense of peace. There was nowhere else to go, nowhere else I needed to be. This silent, still sunset was perfect.

Settled at last into the stillness, I started to laugh at myself. I laughed because I realized what I'd been doing. I had filled the entire day with activity, plans and achievements. The driven, goal-orientated part of me had completely taken over the experience, and it turned out to be ill suited to a day of silence and fasting, because somehow I missed the whole show. I missed the sun going up in the sky, the birds soaring overhead, the smell of the sage at the side of the path, the rocks silently looking on. I missed this beauty all around me. I missed it all because I was so afraid of the empty space. Yet, finally, here I was in Stillness, and it was all I had wanted, all along. This peace and emptiness and tranquility, present all around us, every moment, just waiting for us to turn towards it.

The Nature of Stillness

Doors and windows are cut in the walls of a house.
And because they are empty spaces we are able to use them.
Therefore on the one hand we have the benefit of existence.
And on the other, we make use of non-existence.

– LAO TZU

We live in a universe that is almost entirely empty space. Admittedly, much of our attention is fixed on matter: our beautiful blue-green planet and the oceans, plants and animals it houses; the sun that we circle, the moon, stars and other fiery, molten, solid and gaseous planets that circle the sun with us. Yet between these tangible, physical forms is an expanse of empty space far vaster than all these planets and stars put together. Scientists call it the quantum vacuum, a term the *Oxford English Dictionary* defines as 'a state devoid of ordinary matter'.[7] This vacuum is by far the largest part of our universe, galaxy and solar system.

As humans, we echo this universal ratio of matter to emptiness. The atom is 99.99 per cent empty, and we are made up of atoms. So it follows that we humans are 99.99 per cent empty. Cosmologist Brian Swimme captures the wonder of this in *The Universe Is a Green Dragon*:

> Emptiness permeates you. You are more fecund emptiness then you are created particles. We can see this by examining one of your atoms. If you take a single atom and make it as large as the Yankee Stadium, it would consist almost entirely of empty space. The centre of the atom, the nucleus, would be smaller than a baseball sitting out in centre field. The outer parts of the atom would be tiny gnats buzzing around at an altitude higher than any pop fly Babe Ruth ever hit. And between the baseball and the gnats? Nothingness. All empty. You are more emptiness than anything else. Indeed, if all the space were taken out of you, you would be a million times smaller than the smallest grain of sand.[8]

Yet this emptiness isn't so empty after all. One of the amazing discoveries of the 20th century is that the quantum vacuum is not an absolute void. Rather, it's a kind of force field, what scientists call a 'space–time foam', an energy field full of potentiality. We know this because particles appear and disappear within this space. As Professor Paul Davies writes in *The Last Three Minutes*, 'virtual particles in the quantum vacuum receive some of the (vacuum energy) and get promoted to real particlehood.'[9] So particles literally come from nonexistence into existence – and then disappear again – from the seeming emptiness of the vacuum. What seems to be empty space is actually pure generativity, an empty-full vacuum where life foams into existence and out again.

Perhaps, then, the same law applies to our human world? Perhaps from Stillness, new structures, identities and possibilities can foam into existence? If so, this offers new insight into the emptiness of the Threshold in the journey of change. In these moments, with our lives hollowed out, empty of structure, activity and a clear sense of identity, we too may discover the creativity of the void. If we resist the temptation to collapse back into the familiarity of our old ways and stay with the emptiness of the Threshold, we too can emerge into a new world.

Even when our lives are full and busy, we can still find Stillness within us in every moment. It is the creative void within us – the empty space within our cells, the quantum vacuum within our bodies. It rests inside, available to us anytime, anywhere. We access it by closing our eyes, bringing our awareness inside and settling into ourselves. Turning our gaze to our inner self, we consciously empty ourselves out and give ourselves to the Stillness within.

Resting in this inner Stillness, we see our lives, our feelings and our choices with new eyes. These eyes are the eyes of the Witness: calm, clear, present and objective. As a witness to our own lives, we are alert and attentive to everything that is happening within and around us. We can turn the gaze of this inner witness deep within ourselves or wide across the planes of the universe. Wherever that gaze settles, on whatever person, situation, feeling or decision, it penetrates to the essence of it. Anchored in inner Stillness, able to see things exactly the way they are, we come fully into the present moment.

Sometimes, what we encounter in the stillness brings peace and transcendence; other times, it can be distinctly less blissful. Stillness brings us to what is. Sometimes that is joy; other times it is grief. Sometimes it is trust; other times it is fear. Sometimes it is certainty; other times it is the unknown or unknowable. Stillness makes no judgment of what we find. It simply witnesses and acknowledges whatever shows up and welcomes it as a part of our reality.

As the judgments and preferences of our ego fade away, we come into contact with life in a much deeper, richer way. We allow it to be what it is without needing to change it. We make space for all the colours of life and all the variety of human experience. As we do so, we develop a capacity to hold more of life. We become richer, fuller, deeper, more connected and more available to life and its experiences. Grounded in Stillness, we follow Tibetan lama Nyoshul Khen Rinpoche's invitation, as quoted by Sogyal Rinpoche:

> *Rest in natural great peace this exhausted mind,*
> *Beaten helpless by karma and neurotic thoughts*
> *Like the relentless fury of the pounding waves*
> *In the infinite ocean of samsara.*
> *Rest in natural great peace.*[10]

Reclaiming Stillness

One's action ought to come out of an achieved stillness:
not to be a mere rushing on.

– D H LAWRENCE

Strange, then, that as creatures of primarily empty space, we have such an allergy to emptiness. In fact, we rarely encounter it in our busy modern world. Instead, our lives are fast and full, packed with activity, noise and stimulation. We take only a few weeks of vacation a year. Sunday as a 'day of rest' has long gone, and now we fill our weekends with shopping, chores, life-admin and social commitments. At work, we rush from one meeting to the next, filling the spaces with hundreds of e-mails and long to-do lists. Around the edges of our 9-to-5 day (or 8-to-8 day), we squeeze in more activity and more stimulation: e-mails, phone calls, newspapers, business journals, surfing the internet, Facebook, TV, sports, socializing and personal commitments. All the while, our senses are bombarded with stimulus: billboards, music, sirens, announcements, traffic and other background noise in our fast-paced world. 'I'm too busy to meditate,' we tell ourselves as we rush through our day in a frenzy of activity. 'We don't have time to postpone this decision,' we conclude in meetings, even when we know that the decision is really not clear and that moving to action is premature and potentially destructive. 'Yes, I have a fever, but I can't take the day off,' we tell our partner as we push our bodies into overdrive and struggle on through exhaustion or burn-out. Making space for Stillness in our hectic, chaotic lives can often seem unrealistic or, worse, just another thing on the to-do list.

Stillness is equally absent from the bigger cycles of our working lives. There, too, we plunge from one phase to the next, with little time for reflection and rest in between. We do have some processes for review and consolidation: market research presentations to analyse the success of a launch; year-end conferences to share results and celebrate successes; client presentations to present results and capture learnings; annual performance reviews and appraisals to reflect on what we've achieved and what aspects of our leadership we need to develop. These structures offer just the faintest promise of Stillness. Yet they tend to be relatively superficial and rushed, missing the time and space for deeper contemplation of the experience, challenges and learnings.

Transitional moments between one phase of our career and the next are also glossed over. Moving from student to graduate trainee, trainee to manager, manager to team leader or partner, partner to CEO, CEO to retirement, do we stop to pause and reflect on the phase we're leaving and the phase we're moving into? Do we take time to ask: *Who have I been in this phase of my career? What has success looked like? What's calling me into the next phase? What habits, beliefs and perspectives do I need to move towards to fully step into this new phase? What will sucess look like in this next phase of my life and leadership?* Rushing between one phase and the next, we miss the opportunity of turning inside to seek out insight into these transformational questions.

Without access to Stillness, we tend to rush compulsively from one goal to the next. Often it feels as though something 'out there' is tugging at us, whispering with alluring promises of *more* and *better*. For some of us that something is money, for others it is status, promotion, recognition, a new house, a new lover, a new career. There is nothing wrong with dreams, visions or goals. In fact, they are an extremely valuable part of life. The problem comes when we find ourselves drawn into compulsive activity, driven by a sense of urgency, panic and stress that doesn't go away, even when we get what we wanted.

Somewhere inside us, an unconscious program runs in our head, saying: 'When I have that car/house/relationship/job I will be happy,' 'When I have the next promotion I will take a holiday,' 'When I've achieved this goal I will take a break.' And so we run faster and faster into life, mapping out the next stage and the next, and often failing to acknowledge and enjoy the very place we are already at.

My client and friend David Osborn was an example of this. He is one of the most externally successful people I know: an entrepreneur who has generated a multi-million-dollar business in real estate. Yet no matter how successful he became, he was never satisfied. He told me 'Making $1 million a year for the first time felt no different from making $100,000 a year. Sure, I had a nice house and a better car, which I definitely appreciated. But mostly they just blended into the background of my life, whilst my attention turned to newer goals. For ten years, I never looked back, only forwards. Wherever I was I had more to do, further to go, higher to reach. Rather than celebrating earning $1 million a year, I focused on how I could earn $2 million a year. No matter how well I did, I was permanently dissatisfied.'

It took his father getting mortally sick for David to break out of this cycle of perpetual desire. He chose to take time out from work to care for his dad, which meant letting go of many of his responsibilities and delegating more. When his father died, a couple of years later, David faced a life with more empty space than he'd ever known. It took great courage for him to stay with that emptiness, rather than filling it up again with work activity. As he did so, his relationship to success began to shift, and for the first time in years, he was able to appreciate just how far he'd already come. In the emptiness of the Threshold, new questions appeared. What drove him was no longer the question of: *How can I earn more money and be more successful?* Instead, it was: *What do I really want? And how can I move towards that in my life?* Listening to these deeper longings drew David beyond a desire for wealth and into a new relationship with success, money and life.

As David's story shows, we are not pre-disposed to seek out Stillness and in the modern, western world we are rarely encouraged to do so. So we have to learn for ourselves when to seek out the creativity of empty space. Here are some symptoms that may indicate a need for more Stillness in your life.

* Being busy, but not fully enjoying or appreciating your achievements
* Exhaustion – feeling run down, depleted, with no energy for your current life or future dreams
* The tendency to blow up (or break down) at the slightest provocation
* Living on auto-pilot, too busy to stop and reflect on where you are and where you're headed
* An absence of creativity in your life
* A tendency to stay busy and move fast – even when that's not necessary (for example, on holiday)
* A longing for something you can't quite name – and that won't be satisfied by yet another payrise, promotion, ice cream, car, relationship or whatever else has silenced that longing in the past

If any of these perspectives and behaviours resonate, it may be time to turn inside and make space for pause, reflection and rest. There, in the inner and outer emptiness, you may begin to find a new relationship with Stillness.

The Gifts of Stillness

*It is the stillness that will save and transform
the world.*

– ECKHART TOLLE

When we stop running from the emptiness and turn into it, we discover its gifts. As we've already touched on, one of these gifts is a capacity to see things exactly as they are, to witness our lives through objective eyes. The path of Stillness also leads us to two other important gifts – creativity and productivity.

Just as the quantum vacuum generates life from seeming emptiness, Stillness can support creative breakthroughs in our own lives and work. As inventor Nikola Tesla said, 'The mind is sharper and keener in seclusion and uninterrupted solitude. No big laboratory is needed in which to think. Originality thrives in seclusion free of outside influences beating upon us to cripple the creative mind. Be alone, that is the secret of invention; be alone, that is when ideas are born.'[11] Creating periods of silence and solitude in our working lives, in balance with times of activity and connection, is a powerful path to success.

Rachael Kessler tells a story of the creativity of Stillness in her book *The Soul of Education*. She shares the experience of Colleen Conrad, a class teacher with one of the most challenging classes in her school: low-skilled, high-risk students who had no desire to be there. Into this already challenging environment came disruption. In the middle of the school term, Colleen had to have surgery, which took her away from school for three weeks. When she came back, she found the class in chaos: 'The group lost all feeling of community. They created a disruptive, anti-social community that kept any learning from taking place.'

What to do with this disruption? Overlook it? Judge it? Try to get rid of it? Blame the kids, and give up on them? Colleen took an unconventional approach. First, she named the challenge, sharing how disappointed she was and telling the class that there was no way she could support their learning with this level of negative behaviour. Then she focused on what she wanted. 'I told them I needed us to pull together once again as a positive community. But no one was ready to do that – they had slid into thinking that failure was inevitable.' So, Colleen took a radical step. She invited the class to spend one full week in silence. This was not a punishment. Rather, the silence was offered as a gift, 'an opportunity to decide what our common direction would become.'

Staying with the silence was challenging – even for Colleen. 'It was hard for me to participate in such extended silence, because I believe so strongly in interactive learning. However, I also believed we would never form a community unless we took time to reflect on our vision and goals.' At the end of the week of silence, the class came into a circle to share what they had learned. Several of them said they liked the silence – that it was easier to concentrate and they enjoyed having space for themselves. Yet the silence also showed them how much they valued and wanted interaction with Colleen and each other. Through the experience, the class reset their direction and created a shared set of values and guidelines on how to be as a community. 'The students basically reestablished class norms,' Colleen explained, discovering what kind of an environment they needed and how they could participate in creating that. They emerged, on the other side of Stillness, into a new world.[12]

We often fear that Stillness will make us ineffective; yet in reality the opposite is true. Paolo Pisano, HR director at Pearson publishers, experienced the productivity of Stillness in a change management project he was working on. The team was under fierce time pressure to make a public announcement about the upcoming changes. It was a complex task, with many different streams of communication that needed to happen in a certain order. So the team was brainstorming how to fit their plan into these tight timings. After lengthy discussions, with the pressure mounting, one of the team suggested that they take a break and come back to the problem the next day. The others agreed. And so they created a space of Stillness.

When the team came back together the next day, they came with fresh eyes. Someone asked: 'Can you remind me about the assumptions we're making about the timelines, and why the start and finish dates are set as they are?' Reviewing the timelines, they realized assumptions they'd made about start and finish times were no longer relevant. They'd been fixed around other events that had since moved. So the challenge changed. They could spread the communication over two weeks, and there was no need to start it quite so urgently. With more time to develop the process, the team was less stressed out; there was less risk of things going wrong and more time to fix them if they did. Just a few hours of Stillness made space for reflection and perspective that ensured the team was running down the right road. Those empty hours were, arguably, the most productive hours of the project.

A number of other examples support this link between Stillness and productivity. In the UK, in the first two months of 1974, the government mandated a three-day week in response to fuel shortages brought on by the coal miners' strike. Commercial users of electricity were only allowed to operate for three consecutive days per week. The experiment lasted two months, ending in March 1974 when Heath's government lost power. Analysts later concluded that national output had dropped only 6 per cent in those months, despite the reduced working hours and 1.5 million people newly unemployed. What, then, is the optimal number of working hours?

An experiment in the USA in 2008 leaves us with similar questions. In June 2008, the state of Utah imposed a mandatory four-day week for all public-sector workers in order to save energy and cut carbon emissions. The Working4Utah program shifted the standard working hours from five 8-hour days to four 10-hour days. This left all state workers with a three-day weekend. By May 2009, more than 50 per cent of employees said they were more productive working a four-day week, and over 75 per cent said they preferred the new arrangement. Equally impressive, the four-day week helped reduce carbon emissions by 4,546 metric tons, other greenhouse gas emissions by 8,000 tons and petrol consumption by 744,000 gallons. Both these examples form part of a 2010 report by the British think-tank New Economic Forum (NEF), which argues the case for a standard 21-hour working week. Perhaps, as they suggest, this kind of dramatic shift in our working patterns is the only way to truly address economic, social and environmental problems of the 21st century? Perhaps making more time for Stillness could resolve some of these 'urgent inter-linked problems: overwork, unemployment, over-consumption, high carbon emissions, low well-being, entrenched inequalities, and the lack of time to live sustainably, to care for each other, and simply to enjoy life'?[13]

Through the lens of Stillness, we redefine *productivity*. In the past, productivity was simply producing as much 'stuff' as possible, with as little effort as possible. The *Oxford English Dictionary* (OED) summarises this as: 'the effectiveness of productive effort, especially in industry, as measured in terms of the rate of output (of goods, products, etc.) per unit of input (of labour, materials, equipment, etc.)'.[14] This linear definition made sense in the industrial age, when business was primarily about running efficient production lines. But modern business is not merely about operating efficient production lines. Modern business requires creative ideas, inventiveness, innovation, vision and imaginative ways of engaging the world around us. Surely the outputs we need are radically creative solutions to the challenges of our time – not just more stuff, produced more quickly? And surely the measure of success is the quality of the goods and services (not to mention lives and societies) we are generating – not just the quantity? Perhaps, then, a more contemporary and useful definition of *productiveness* is: 'richness of output; fertility, fruitfulness'.[15]

Reclaiming Stillness doesn't mean abandoning all activity or ceasing to produce. It means finding a healthier relationship between activity and reflection, doing and being. These stories and statistics remind us that productivity does not increase exponentially with time and activity. The body has rhythms, as does the soul, and these rhythms include Stillness. Like the land, humans need fallow periods for Stillness to replenish the soil of our lives. When we listen to these inner rhythms and align our working lives with them, we learn to value contemplation, emptiness and rest as deeply as we value activity. We get more done, more consciously.

Remembering Stillness and its gifts shakes the very foundations of our post-industrial working world. Given what we're discovering about creativity and Stillness, does it really make sense to work 9 to 5 (or 8 to 8), five days a week? If we were really to acknowledge and honour the truth that creativity thrives in empty space, how would we design our working lives? How could we build Stillness into all areas of work: from the overall structure of the working week, through the design of brainstorming, training sessions or client meetings, to our everyday habits and choices? And how could we support ourselves, each other and our organizations through the inevitable disorientation of the Threshold in our Journeys of transformation?

The answers are not yet clear. As visionary and courageous leaders, all we can do is lean into the Stillness, and listen there, in the uncertainty, to the still, calm wisdom of our soul.

Making Space for Stillness
Richard Hytner, Saatchi & Saatchi

Richard Hytner is deputy chairman of Saatchi & Saatchi, one of the largest and most highly regarded advertising agencies in the world. He is smart, successful and has the brightest, clearest blue eyes I've ever come across in a business leader. When you meet him, you know at once: *this man is alive*. He's also a man who knows about Stillness.

It wasn't always that way. In fact, Richard's journey into Stillness was triggered by the stress and noise of his manic, busy life. 'Running a company, I ended up constantly at the beck and call of other people, constantly ready to put out some fire or other. And so I found myself experiencing this constant, constant drag into noise and activity and discord. I didn't really know it at the time, but looking back I can see I was ridiculously stressed.' Living in this chaotic way became so familiar that Richard couldn't even rest when he was away on holiday. 'It was so bad that my wife would actually manufacture things for me to do. Literally from the minute I got up, she'd give me this list of things to keep me busy. And I'd be happy again! But deep down I knew that it wasn't sustainable or good for me.'

This went on for 12 years. It was uncomfortable and tiring, but it was also familiar. Yet, feeling a sense of growing desperation, Richard began looking for a way to turn the noise off. In the end, the path found him. His wife, Rosie, read an article by a journalist she had once worked for. The article was about the need for meditation, and as he read it he recognized the triggers and characteristics in himself. There was a phone number, and that was it . . . Richard signed up to learn meditation.

'At first, things got worse. I thought it was going to beat me. I felt this extraordinary claustrophobia, and I was so up and down. I can feel it now. I think that was just years of pent-up tension and stress that I hadn't given an outlet, so that when I created space it all came pouring out. It was terrifying, actually. And I can't remember exactly when that turned from that horrendous feeling to almost the opposite: complete euphoria. But it did. The meditation schools talk about this with the image of the seabed. When we first open to Stillness, we kick up all the cloudy, murky feelings at the bottom of the seabed. Yet over time, these feelings settle and a new level of clarity emerges.'

Even within the demands of his current role, as deputy chairman of Saatchi & Saatchi, Richard now meditates twice a day, without fail. As he points out, 'It's not always easy at work. Organizations don't make it easy. We have all these spaces for activity, all these meeting rooms – but there are no spaces for Stillness. And even if we did have a meditation room, I'm not sure that people would use it. People might do yoga, because that's activity and tracksuits. But meditation? I think people worry that other people will think they are not busy enough – and therefore not doing an important job. There are just years and years of conditioning that push us into this high testosterone approach to work where we have to "do more" to prove ourselves. But once you know that you're at your best in this stillness, you don't allow yourself to get vulnerable to volume and nonsense and noise. And actually you learn to distrust it.' So now when Richard feels himself being drawn into that feeling, a voice inside of him says, 'Watch out . . . pause.' And so he takes a step back and waits until he can feel connection with that calm inner space again.

Learning to find a place of inner Stillness amid the busyness of his life transformed Richard's life, work and leadership. He's still successful – in fact, he's arguably more successful. He still gets things done. He still achieves and delivers results. He still leads teams. Yet he does all these things more consciously. His actions come from a deeper place of awareness. And this has brought many gifts to his own career and to the teams he works with.

'For me, the gift of Stillness is creativity. Yes, there are moments when you need tension, conflict and deadlines for creativity. But for me personally, I find I tend to be more free-flowing and fertile when I am in Stillness. I also find I am more productive. My team is a fast-paced, energetic, high-octane team. We overdeliver. We get lots done, but not in that kind of manic, disorganized, chaotic, high-testosterone way. That's the paradox. We get more done, more quickly, more effectively – more calmly.'

Speed and Stillness at Work

Kate Franklin, HR Professional

Kate Franklin is a brilliant coach whose specialty is offering what she calls 'clear-head coaching' to leaders in fast-paced organizations. Focused and professional, Kate is also calm and present.

Stillness was something Kate also had to learn. At the age of 30, she had just been promoted to head of leadership development for a large insurance company in London. Although she was successful, highly regarded and capable, under the surface things didn't look so pretty. She had extremely high standards, which meant whilst most people left the office at 5:30pm, she was routinely still there at 9:30pm. As she describes it, 'I was constantly busy, stressed and in a rush. The only thing that kept me going was caffeine.' Meanwhile, at home, she was having trouble sleeping. She cried at night and woke up tearful and stressed because she'd only slept an hour. On Sunday lunchtimes, she would find herself in tears, overwhelmed and anxious about the week ahead. 'I was shattered and run down. Yet I believed these were the sacrifices you had to make to be successful.'

A few weeks after Kate's promotion, her new boss took her aside. 'I'm confused. You're clearly doing well here. And yet you seem so anxious and stressed. What's going on?' she asked. Refusing to accept Kate's explanation that 'this is just how I am', she encouraged her to work with a leadership coach. And through that experience, everything changed.

'Coaching gave me time and space for reflection – for Stillness. From that Stillness, my coach helped me to unpick all the assumptions that were leading me to work so obsessively.' One by one, Kate took these assumptions apart and redefined what 'good' looked like. Equally important, she explored why she was feeling anxious so often. She realized that her anxiety was a clever way of ensuring that people would forgive her when she broke promises or showed up late for a family gathering or social event. 'It was a way of ensuring that I didn't have to face the consequences of my fast, work-focused life.'

Kate wanted to take responsibility for her choices and actions rather than using anxiety to justify them. That meant she needed to slow down and create enough Stillness to hear and acknowledge her own needs. She introduced new structures to help her cultivate this Stillness: making time for exercise, learning meditation, prioritizing time alone and starting a practice of journaling. At the same time, she restructured her work life, cutting back her hours to a strict 9:30am to 5:30pm. She pushed back when people made requests, challenging their urgency and importance. It was scary. Yet to her surprise, she ended up doing a better job. That year, for the first time ever, she got the company's top performance rating – Outstanding.

Four years later, Kate is still learning to weave together speed and Stillness. 'I haven't lost my drive, ambition and appetite for more. There are times when it feels great to step into the speed, excitement and possibility of that driven part of me. But I also appreciate Stillness now. I appreciate the ability to enjoy doing just one thing at a time; to really focus, listen and engage.' Through her own personal development and her work with clients, Kate is learning, over and over, the value of this place of inner calm. 'It's like a pool in a forest, where beautiful animals come for water. But they only come when we are quiet and still. And the beauty of this Stillness is a gift I can give myself, every day.'

Source: My interviews with Richard Hytner and Kate Franklin

PRACTICE # 2

24-Hour Solo

In our fast-paced modern lives, we have to make a conscious decision to create periods of Stillness. One way of doing this is to set aside 24 hours to spend alone, in silent reflection. I've challenged many of my clients with this task (or a variation of it) and have found that it consistently brings rich experiences and insights. If you feel drawn to experiment with this practice (even if the idea repels or terrifies you!), here are a few guidelines.

First: cut off connection to and stimulation from the outside world (as much as you can), leaving behind TV, mobile phone, newspapers, internet and books. It's fine to journal, draw, daydream and engage with Curiosity Walks (outlined below) or any other activity where insight emerges from within. Traditionally, in a 24-hour solo we would also leave behind the stimulus of the city, with its billboards, people, advertising, noise and hustle, and drop into a deeper connection with ourselves through the quieter solitude of the wilderness. However, many of my clients have experimented with a 24-hour solo in London or other large cities and have had powerful experiences and insights. Do what feels right to you.

Second: find a good place for your solo. If you live alone, you may like to simply stay home. If you have a family, it may be harder to find a private space. Some people camp out in the wilderness, others find a room in their home and stay there. Again, do what feels right for you. Let people know where you are and that you will not be contactable for the next 24 hours. Set an emergency protocol – what they should do if they don't hear from you by an agreed time (just in case!).

Third: decide if you want to include a fast as part of your solo. It's not necessary, but it can be a useful way to heighten emotional sensitivity and

45

deepen the connection with your inner world. If you do fast, make sure you drink plenty of water – at least a gallon (three and a half to four litres) a day.

Note: If you have any doubts about fasting safely, or about your readiness for any aspect of the solo, consult an expert or your medical practitioner before you begin.

Once you've established the parameters, you're ready to drop in to the experience.

1. Set a clear **intention** for your solo time. It could be to mark a transition in your life – between one role and the next, one way of being and another, an old identity and something new, one life phase and the next. Or it could be to get insight into a particular challenge, question or concern in your work or personal life. Write your intention clearly in your journal.

2. When it's time to begin the 24-hour solo, **open the space**. This can be as simple or elaborate as you like – lighting a candle, crossing a threshold, stating your intent out loud. Spend time creating a physical space that supports, nurtures and inspires you. You might like to begin your solo by gathering objects from the natural or human world that inspire and support your intention.

3. **Let the experience 'do' you.** You don't need a plan for your 24 hours – in fact, it's best not to have one. Let your intuition guide you from one moment to the next. Stay present with every feeling, experience and insight that emerges. You might spend time with a vivid dream you've recently had, or daydream or journal. You might also like to practise a Curiosity Walk (outlined below). Most importantly, let go of *doing* and open to *being*.

4. When the 24 hours comes to an end, **mark the Threshold back into your daily life.** Again, you can do this as simply or elaborately as you like – perhaps speaking your discoveries, insight and gratitude out loud and closing the space ceremonially by blowing out a candle or wiping away outer traces of your

experience in your home or the natural world.

5. Be aware that the **experience may continue** even after you mark the end of your 24 hours. Be gentle with yourself and give yourself plenty of space and time to transition back into your routines and commitments. Pay attention to your dreams and any 'chance encounters' over the next days and weeks. They may have insights to offer that build or deepen the insights you gathered through your solo experience.

6. If it feels right, **share your experience** with someone else – perhaps a partner or a coach. Make sure you create an environment where you can take your time, and make it clear what role you'd like the other person to play: simply to witness your story? To mirror it back? To offer insight?

7. Spend some time clarifying any **commitments** that you want to make. Think about how you want to be held accountable to those commitments, and whether you need to ask anyone else to support you in this. One very simple way to keep your experience alive is to connect back to it every morning for the next month and ask yourself: *What's one thing I can do today to move my dream forwards?* Do it.

Curiosity Walk

A Curiosity Walk is a powerful and natural part of a solo experience, especially when that experience includes time in the natural world. It can also work as a shorter, stand-alone experience.

Curiosity Walk works on the basis that all of life is connected – that nature and human nature follow the same laws and that some part of life has already faced and resolved almost every challenge we face. When we move into the world with an open mind and heart and allow our curiosity to lead us, we are drawn towards places, creatures and experiences that mirror the questions and challenges of our own lives. This helps us gain new insight, perspective and understanding.

Here's how to experiment with this practice.

1. Determine your question or **intention** for the walk. This could be as large or small as you want. Again, you might want to explore some of the questions we've raised – for example, *What is dying in my life right now?* – or ask a more general question such as *What's my relationship to Stillness?*

2. **Decide where your walk will start and finish.** Ideally, this should be the same place, and wherever you choose will become the Threshold. Your threshold might be a certain tree, a crack in the paving stones or sidewalk, your office door, a gate, an archway, the beginning of a trail or any other memorable landmark.

3. As you set out on your walk, **mark the threshold** consciously. Pause just before you cross the threshold, and clearly state your intention – either out loud or quietly in your head, depending on where you are and how crazy you're willing to feel! Ask life to bring you insight around this question. Then centre yourself, consciously opening to receive insight and letting go of any hopes, fears or expectations about what you might discover – and step across the threshold.

4. **Begin walking**. Generally it's a good idea to move slowly and mindfully. Notice what captures your attention. Spend time with it – whether it's a rock, a tree, a particular plant, a bird, an animal, a hole in the ground – whatever it is that pulls your curiosity towards it. Listen to your intuition and allow it to guide you, letting you know which way to walk, when it's time to stop or pause for deeper reflection or to connect more fully with a particular being in the natural world. There are no rules, just let yourself be moved through the walk.

5. When it feels time, **come back to where you started**. Before you

cross back over the Threshold, close your eyes and let the journey settle in your awareness and your body. Feel your gratitude for any insights and experiences you had, whatever they were, no matter how dramatic or subtle. Sometimes it helps to run through the different stages of the journey in your mind or speak out loud what you learned before you cross the Threshold (your office door, tree, or crack in the sidewalk).

6. Before you move back into the day's activity, **capture the journey in your journal**. You might write it as a story, draw pictures of the significant moments and encounters or simply write a few key words about the insights you were given. If you're working as a group, come together in a circle and **share stories**, speaking to the essence of the experience and listening deeply for the common threads and insights across the different stories within the group.

7. Ask yourself if there is any action or **commitment** that you need to take based on the insights you got from the walk. If so, take it.

CHAPTER 3

Intuition

Listening Deeply

*You have to leave the city of your comfort
and go into the wilderness of your intuition*

. . .

*what you'll discover will be wonderful.
What you'll discover is yourself.*

– ALAN ALDA–

And so from the Stillness we open to Intuition:
listening, sensing and feeling
our way into our emerging world.
What future calls to you
through the longings and knowings
of your Intuition?

Discovering Intuition: My Story

After my encounter with Stillness in Lone Pine, I dropped fully into the Threshold of change. For six months, my life lacked any sense of direction. I couldn't see the path, nor where it led. My future was a dark, unknown space, and I had no idea where I was going to be living, what work I would do or even how I was going to fill the next day. In the disorientation of that emptiness, all I could do was follow my curiosity from this moment to the next, and allow my unknown future to draw me towards it that way.

So I began to experiment with a range of workshops and experiences – everything that caught my attention and seemed interesting to me. That included classes in salsa, tango, shamanism, astrology, yoga, poetry, singing, storytelling, dreams and coaching. There was no plan, no sense of how I'd use these teachings, just a curiosity to learn and expose myself to a wide range of theories, philosophies and ways of seeing the world.

Somewhere within that journey of discovery, I found myself in Sacramento, California, on a workshop with Carolyn Conger PhD, a psychologist and intuitive teacher I'd heard about through Brugh Joy. From the very first time I heard her name and listened to some of the stories of her intuitive abilities, I knew I wanted to meet her. There was no logical explanation – after all, she was based on the west coast of America and I was living in Argentina, a twelve-hour, $1,000 flight away. Yet, regardless of the logistical barriers, there was solidity to the longing – a calm, deep, grounded feeling that this was a woman I wanted to meet. So I signed up for her week-long residential workshop on Creativity & Intuition and made my way to California once more. And I found myself face to face with Carolyn Conger, a woman who would become my mentor for the next three years and a dear friend for many more.

The workshop was held on what may be one of the most beautiful pieces of land in the world – a ranch near Grass Valley, with green, rolling hills, ancient oak trees and a California sky. We were a small group of eight, all ready to dive deeply into our personal journeys through meditation, writing, dream work, dance, song, poetry and time on the land. I enjoyed all these practices, but it was our evening sessions that really broke me into my intuition.

Our sessions took place in a big open barn, whose concrete floor was softened with our circle of armchairs and the twinkling of fairylights and candles. It was the first evening, and we sat in silence, dropping into a stiller place after the buzz and chatter of dinner. As the energy of the group settled, Carolyn began to speak. 'We're going to practise using intuition with other people. In a moment, Mary[16] is going to come into the circle and I want you to use your intuition to tune in to her energy. I'll give you questions to focus on, and you can share your insights and answers. I've asked Mary to stay silent and not to react in any way to what you say. At the end, she'll give you feedback. Feel free to use the tarot cards I gave you, if that's helpful. Otherwise, just trust whatever images, words or sensations arise.'

I looked at Carolyn with disbelief. She wanted us to *what*? To share personal information about someone else, based on absolutely no facts, out loud, in front of everyone? I wanted to fall through the floor and disappear right then. Yet despite my terror, the idea also intrigued me. Could this work? Might I be able to connect energetically to another person and use my intuition to get a sense for who she was and what she wanted? Was that really possible?

Mary came into the room, and Carolyn started suggesting questions. *What was this person like as a child?* I closed my eyes and allowed my racing mind to settle. Breathing deeply, I turned my attention towards the Stillness at my centre and brought Mary's silent presence into my awareness. I saw a picture of a young girl with plaits, maybe age seven or eight, running through a wide, open field. There was a sense of space, freedom, playfulness. Watching the scene in my mind, I noticed an old wooden gate. It seemed that the little girl would go up to the gate, but not beyond it. I didn't know what that meant – but it seemed significant.

I opened my eyes again. Other people were sharing insights and feelings. One of the girls in the group had a whole storyboard of tarot cards laid out in front of her and was flipping confidently through yet more cards. I swallowed hard. Really, was I going to share what I'd felt and seen? Did it make any sense? What if it was totally irrelevant or just plain wrong? The idea of sharing these intuitions made me feel incredibly exposed. 'Just throw it out there,' I coaxed myself. 'It doesn't matter if it's all wrong – throw it out there anyway.' So I took a deep breath and offered my insights to the silent Mary.

We continued like this for close to an hour, as Carolyn offered other questions for us to explore. *What are Mary's gifts? What challenges is she facing in her life right now? What about her health?* As I relaxed into this surreal experience, I began to experiment. Focusing on challenges, I picked a tarot card. It was The Priestess. Putting aside the words on the card, as Carolyn advised, I focused on the image alone. I saw a woman who was filled with energy and movement in her upper body, yet with feet and legs of stone. I nodded silently as everything else fell away and just this piece of the picture came into focus. 'The picture I've drawn is a woman with legs of stone,' I shared. 'It seems like you're stuck, not able to move forwards in your life right now.' Later, tuning in to health, I tried another technique: simply scanning the body in my mind, with my eyes closed and my attention in the Stillness within me. My attention was drawn to the lower belly – to a sense of darkness around the liver. So I shared what I saw.

By the end of that hour, the room was filled with a sense of calm, concentration and connection. I'd relaxed into the experience, putting aside my worries about making a mistake, and it seemed the other participants had too. Then, with fairylights still twinkling in the background, Mary shared the story of her life – her childhood, where she was right now and the challenges she faced. She gave feedback on some of the intuitive offerings we'd given – especially those that had really resonated. It turned out that she had grown up on a farm and had spent many years running through open fields. But she had also grown up with strict religious teachings of right and wrong, which left her afraid to explore life too widely – hence the gate. Mary did indeed feel stuck right now, unsure what direction to take for this next phase of her life. To my amazement, it also turned out she had Hepatitis B – which explained why her liver was showing up as a focal point for her health.

In that bare, magical barn, I was cracked open to the power of Intuition. We repeated the same process every night, and with each reading my confidence grew. I began to realize just how much information is available to us, when we dare to trust and speak our intuition. What I learned in those still, silent evenings became the foundation for all my later work in coaching and workshop facilitation, where intuitively 'reading' a leader or a room full of leaders made the difference between superficial engagement and a truly insightful conversation.

The Nature of Intuition

Your mind knows only some things.
Your inner voice, your instinct, knows everything.
If you listen to what you know instinctively,
it will always lead you down the right path.

– HENRY WINKLER

Intuition is, by its nature, difficult to define. Definitions belong to a rational, concrete, measurable world; Intuition does not. Even Carl Jung, 20th-century psychologist, declared that 'because in the main intuition is an unconscious process, its nature is very difficult to grasp.'[17] Those who do try to define it (and there have been many, especially in the last 50 years), attempt to do so in über-rational terms that lose the very essence of Intuition.[18] Intuition taps into the mystery of life, and that mystery is something we may never fully understand or define. Still, an exploration of Intuition can be rich and revealing. So as we move into this chapter, set aside the rational mind and its tendency to define and delineate, and open to a more subtle and experiential relationship with Intuition and its gifts.

To start to get a sense of Intuition, we can turn to the Four Elements: Earth, Water, Air and Fire. The Four Elements have been used across time and across cultures as a way of understanding and mapping the different aspects of human beings. They show up in China, India, ancient Greece and Japan, as well as in astrology and indigenous traditions across the world. Each model is unique, yet they also share common ground. In all cases, each of the four (or sometimes five) elements corresponds to a different aspect of life, and by extension, the human being. Taking the astrological model as an example, Earth is the body – concrete, physical, solid form. It has the slowest vibration. After Earth comes Water and the realm of feeling. Like water, feelings are changeable – mild like a light rain, calm like the surface of a lake or ferocious like a pounding ocean – as well as powerful and transformative. Next comes Air: quick-moving, invisible connector that corresponds to thinking and the rational mind. Finally, we have Fire. Fire is sacred, life-giving, a source of light, warmth and comfort. It is powerful and transformational in its own way, with an ability to both create and destroy. In the astrological model of the Four Elements, it corresponds to soul or spirit.

Intuition belongs with Fire and the soul. Used in this sense, *soul* is 'the spiritual part of man in contrast to the purely physical'.[19] This is not a religious belief. It's simply the awareness that humans (and life) have an energetic component, as well as a physical one. These energies are timeless patterns, building blocks of our reality that are expressed and re-expressed across generations. Together, they form an invisible, mythical realm: an energetic reality that sits behind and within the concrete forms of physical reality.

This is not a new idea. As far back as the 5th century BC, Plato wrote about these patterns, referring to them as *ideas* or *forms*: 'perfect patterns embedded in the very nature of things'.[20] According to Plato's philosophy, all physical life is derived from these unseen, universal, timeless patterns. A similar philosophy forms the basis of the Greek Pantheon, where the gods and goddesses embody these different patterns of life: Hera, the jealous wife; Zeus, the ruler; Aphrodite, the lover; Ares, the warrior. In Tarot, these universal patterns are the different cards: Lover, Priestess, Emperor, Magician. In shamanic traditions, they are the elements of non-ordinary reality – a mythical realm that we can access only through the inner world. Carl Jung labelled them *archetypes*, which literally translates as 'first patterns'. For Jung, archetypes are 'the accumulated experience of organic life in general, a million times repeated and condensed into types.'[21] All these philosophies and models are expressions of a similar understanding: that patterns of energy dance behind and within our physical reality, and that these patterns exist across individuals, cultures, time and space.

Intuition is the way we sense and tap into these universal patterns, or archetypes, within ourselves and our communities. Through an intuitive lens, we look beyond physical form into the invisible, intangible, unconscious patterns of our reality – the undercurrents of our life. Listening to our intuition, we sense the energetic building blocks of each individual soul – its unique patterns, gifts and potential. We also sense the energetic building blocks within a group – the patterns, dynamics, gifts, challenges and potential within the group soul. Looking behind the surface of our physical reality, we ask:

1. What's here right now?

2. What wants to emerge?

3. How can I participate in that emerging reality?

These three questions are the focus of our intuitive attention, and they draw us into the realm of possibility and transformation.

Jung's work on personality types supports this understanding of Intuition. In his essay 'Psychological Types', Jung presents Sensation and Intuition as two complementary, opposite ways of seeing the world. People with a preference for Sensation perceive reality through the five senses: taste, touch, sight, sound, smell. As a result, they are primarily concerned with physical forms that are concrete and measurable. Intuition, on the other hand, is 'the function of unconscious perception'.[22] Where Sensation is concerned with facts, Intuition 'tries to apprehend the widest range of *possibilities*'.[23] It identifies these possibilities by tuning in to and 'reading' patterns, archetypes and unconscious dynamics.

Seen in this way, we could say that Intuition is the voice of our soul, our future self (and our future society) calling to us. This might sound a little strange to Western minds, used to seeing time as a linear, one-way process. In our models of time, only past and present can be measured and understood; the future is an empty space. Seen in this way, life is an empty canvas on which we paint the present, piece by piece. Anything beyond 'now' is unspecified, undefined and unknown. This is one truth; another paradoxical yet equally powerful truth is that the possibilities of the future already exist in the present. They do not yet exist in a tangible form. They are not necessarily experiences we can measure through the five senses. So, with our preference for Sensation, we may overlook or fail to see them. Yet they are there nonetheless, in subtle, energetic form.

In the seed of an oak tree lies the genetic coding and information that determines what kind of a tree this oak will become. The soul is like that seed. It too contains patterns, coding and information about who we are, what we love and what gifts we bring – some of which are conscious and many of which are not. Intuition connects us back to this genetic coding, to the unique programs and patterns of our soul – including those parts of the soul that are not yet conscious. It draws the unconscious parts of our soul to the surface. It connects us to the fullness and potential of our soul, reminding us who we are, what gifts we bring and what life is ours to live. It links our present reality and our future potential.

In his 2005 commencement address to the graduating students at Stanford University, Steve Jobs, founder and CEO of Apple, referred to this as joining the dots. At the age of 17, Jobs had no idea what he wanted to do or become. Unsure how college would support him, and unable to justify the costs to his working-class adoptive parents, he dropped out of Reed College. Sleeping on friends' floors, Jobs found himself in an empty space, with no fixed schedule. In that emptiness, with no formal demands on his time, he started to drop in on the classes that captured his curiosity. One of these was a calligraphy class. Back then, the teenage Jobs had no idea how this class would later play out in his life and his work at Apple. He simply noticed the beautiful calligraphy on posters across campus and followed his intuition to find out more about it.[24]

At the time, taking those classes seemed illogical and impractical. It was only later that the significance became clear. Ten years on, everything Jobs had learned about calligraphy and typography was designed into the Mac, with its multiple typefaces and proportionally spaced fonts. So although at the time it didn't seem very sensible to drop out of formal classes and follow his curiosity and intuition, that decision actually brought Jobs into experiences that would later prove priceless. This is a very typical experience, when following intuition. As Jobs explained to the Stanford graduates, you cannot join the dots looking forwards, only looking backwards. And the challenge is to trust something – whether you call that your gut, destiny, life, karma, or whatever – and to know that somehow the dots will connect in the future.[25] According to Jobs, this approach has never let him down.

When we face choices in our life and work, Intuition acts as an inner compass, pointing us towards the magnetic north of our soul. When we open to our intuition, we are drawn inevitably towards what wants to come into form, what yearns for life, what is struggling to become conscious – the possibilities waiting for us in the future, the unexpressed energies of our soul. Listening to our intuition allows us to look beyond what has been possible and to move towards what is becoming possible. In making the unconscious conscious, Intuition links who we are as leaders, with who we could become as leaders; how we are functioning as a team with how we could potentially function as a team; what's possible in the current market with opportunities becoming possible in our emerging market. It connects the conscious and the not-yet-conscious, the manifest and the not-yet-manifest, ego and soul.

It's not necessarily that Intuition predicts a pre-determined future, nor that our life is irrevocably mapped out, leaving us with no way of shaping or defining it. Rather, it's that we co-create the future with the energies available in the present. Listening to our intuition, we lean our awareness into the present. We notice what captures our attention, what draws our curiosity, what brings us alive – and we follow it. In a sense, we therefore participate in a vibrant field of energies and possibility that exist right here, right now, and that also draw us into the future with their unfolding. In some way, by leaning our awareness into the possibilities that we sense, we charge them up. Seen in this way, the future is not an inanimate space we walk into, but something that is alive, magnetic, charged. This magnetic future draws us towards it through the longings of the soul – and it speaks to us through our intuition.

Reclaiming Intuition

Cease trying to work everything out with your minds.
It will get you nowhere. Live by intuition and inspiration
and let your whole life be Revelation.

– EILEEN CADDY

Intuition is wildly undervalued in our intellectual, rational Western culture. Data from Myers Briggs shows that only 25 per cent of people in the USA and UK prefer Intuition as a way of perceiving reality. The other 75 per cent prefer Sensation.[26] This means that, in the Western world, we tend to pay more attention to outer form and less attention to what lies within, between, or around the edges of that form. We focus on systems and structures, rather than possibilities in our invisible, intuited reality. We pay attention to what is already conscious, rather than what is emerging.

There are a number of side effects of overlooking Intuition and over-emphasizing Sensation. First, seeing 'reality' only in terms of concrete, physical forms makes us a somewhat literal and materialistic society. Our definition of success is to have more, bigger, better 'things', and we often overlook the importance of inner fulfillment. This emphasis on outer, physical forms also means we resist change. Holding onto solid, slow-moving forms (Sensation) we are slow to respond to the quicker movements and changes in the energies of our soul – so we get bogged down, holding rigidly on to familiar forms and structures rather than trusting Intuition to lead us into new possibilities and new ways of being in the world. Whilst the essence of education, health and politics is changing and evolving, we continue to create systems, products and services for the reality that is fading. Failing to lean in to our emerging future, we create me-too innovations and strategies and miss the bigger, riskier opportunities that come when we listen to our intuition.

Even when we do acknowledge our intuition, we are still reluctant to trust it. So we try to post-rationalize it or 'prove it' with facts, figures and rational explanations. This is valuable to some extent; after all, the possibilities of the future *can* be intuited through information available in the present, and using this information to support our intuitions may help us distinguish between what we sense emerging and what we merely desire. Yet to support an intuitive decision in this way requires an intuitive understanding of the facts, which may look less tangible and rigid than rational, unquestionable 'proof'. Trusting and investing in our intuition takes courage.

Intuition arrives softly, a subtle fragrance on a passing breeze. It speaks in a whisper, through subtle sensations, feelings, anxieties, longings and knowings that wait patiently for our attention. In the noise, stimulus and speed of modern life, these hazy whispers can easily get drowned out. Because of this, many people believe they are not intuitive. From my experience with helping teams and leaders develop their intuition, I don't agree. I believe everyone has the ability to be intuitive.

Intuition is like a muscle or an instrument. Anyone can learn to listen to it, just as anyone can build up their triceps or learn to play the violin. Some learn it as children, others don't pick it up until later in life. For some people are 'naturals'. For them, learning comes easily and they simply have to fine-tune their gifts. Others find it less instinctive and have to work harder to develop the skills. In both cases, we get better with practice. Sometimes we neglect Intuition, and it gets rusty and out of tune. Yet when we turn back towards it, pick it up, dust it off, retune it and make time to practise, our intuitive ability comes bouncing back.

What stops us acknowledging Intuition is not that we lack the gift, but rather that we don't know how to listen for it. In other words, we don't create the right conditions to receive its guidance. Hearing Intuition requires an ability to be present in Stillness. In our outer lives, that means developing a practice like yoga, meditation, running, walking, or simply sitting in Stillness, so that we create a space for Intuition to arrive and be heard. In our inner world, it means emptying ourselves of preferences and prejudices. Indigenous traditions speak of this emptying out as a process of becoming a 'Hollow Bone'. That means scraping out the bone marrow of our ego's expectations, desires, fears and becoming a clear, open channel. Through this hollow channel, Intuition can flow, bringing insight, wisdom and truth – expected and unexpected, welcome and unwelcome.

Another block to accessing our intuition is recognizing it when it arrives. Perhaps we are expecting something dramatic and concrete: a vision or a voice that speaks to us. Yet this may not be our way of receiving intuitive information. Intuition comes in many forms, which vary enormously from person to person. Some people see pictures or images – clairvoyance. Others hear a word or sound – clairaudience. Others get physical sensations in the body like a tingling feeling – clairsentience. Others simply get a sense beyond words, sounds or sensation – direct knowing. All of these ways of listening to our intuition are equally valid. There's no right or wrong. The challenge is simply to discover our own particular preference, and then to listen to it.

Even with the right conditions in place, Intuition is not always easy to hear. Sometimes it hovers under the surface of our awareness and we have to actively seek it out. At these times, we can follow a three-part process: PAUSE, CENTRE, SHIFT. First we PAUSE and turn inwards, stopping what we're doing and making space for the intuitive journey. At this stage it often helps to close our eyes and block out the distractions of the outer world. Next, we turn towards our CENTRE. Here, we let go of thoughts and expectations and empty ourselves out to become the Hollow Bone. We drop into a quiet, open space inside: inner Stillness. From this spacious open centre, we SHIFT our attention to the decision, situation or relationship that we need intuitive insight into – and we listen deeply.

When working with Intuition, it's important to have a specific question or intent. Our intuitive radar can pick up all kinds of subtle information from many different sources. Focusing on a specific question or intent turns the radar in a particular direction. Our intuition can then focus on sensations, words, images or sounds that offer insight into that question and filter out all the other information that our unconscious is picking up.

Intuition can support any number of large and small decisions that we take in our everyday business lives. We might use our intuition to explore something very general: *What are my gifts? What brings me alive?* Or our question may be more specific, anchored in a particular moment: *Is it time for a career change – and if so, what is calling me? Is it right to launch this product – and if so, when? Why is my brand in decline? What innovation opportunities are emerging on the horizon? How must we adapt to thrive in a changing world?* The question we ask may even be more specific, supporting daily decisions of our work and lives: *Shall I write this presentation tonight or tomorrow morning? Would it serve me to go to this conference or meeting? Can I trust the results of this market research?* All these questions help us to penetrate below the surface, into the patterns of our unfolding reality.

Sometimes we also want to listen to our intuition about others: *What are the dynamics of this team or relationship? What are the blocks to communication? What is this conflict really about – and how can we resolve it? What does my boss need from me? What do I need from my boss or team? Can I trust this person with such sensitive information? Is this candidate the right person for the job?* If the people are present, we can consciously connect with them by turning our full attention towards them and opening to receive intuitive guidance. If they are not physically present, we can simply call them to mind and connect energetically.

When we actively seek out Intuition, it tends to arrive in stages. With each question, we peel away another layer of insight and get closer to the core. It's a bit like drilling through layers of rock. Quite quickly, we get the first intuitive response. If we want more detail, we simply ask another question, digging deeper and deeper into the picture that is emerging. Slowly we build up a deep and comprehensive view of the person or situation we are intuitively connecting with. When we have a clear insight into the situation, relationship or question, we release our attention and refocus it on another area.

It may be useful to explore an example here. I was working with a client to help her develop her own intuitive abilities. I asked her to use her intuition to get insight into my life, focusing on the question: *Where am I right now?* The first image she saw was of me leaning against a wall. So she shared that image. That didn't mean much to me yet, so I asked her to dig deeper and look for more detail. *What kind of wall is it?* I asked. It is the wall of a house. *Whose house?* It's your house, but it's been abandoned. It is falling apart. *Am I inside or outside?* You're outside, sheltering against the wall. But the house is falling down and it's not really sheltering you. It's just that you're afraid to go out into the open space. *What's inside the house?* I notice the bedroom is empty. You're waiting for someone to come back. I think you're holding onto an old relationship, but the bed is empty and he's gone. *What is possible if I walk away?* Then I see a field full of four-leaf clover. A lot of luck, joy and growth is possible. I see you free and happy. You just need to leave the shelter of the old house.

These images presented a very accurate insight into my life at that point. I was indeed holding on to an old, dead relationship. I was sheltering against a crumbling wall in the empty house of my old worldview. And there were plenty of opportunities waiting for me as soon as I found the courage to walk away. So it was a very precise, intuitive insight into my inner world. As with most intuitive processes, the insight was built up in layers, by asking a series of questions and digging deeper and deeper into the specifics of each image.

Intuition does not speak to us literally; it speaks in the language of symbol. That means each place, object, character, animal and image 'stands for, represents, or denotes something else (not by exact resemblance, but by vague suggestion, or by some accidental or conventional relation)'.[27] In the example I just shared, it wasn't that the walls of my house were literally crumbling. Nor was the vision suggesting that I sell my home and go and live in an open field. Speaking through metaphor, my client's intuition was suggesting that my inner home, my old sense of identity, was dissolving. If I could find the courage to accept that, I could move beyond my current limitations and make room for a more open, spacious way of belonging in the world.

Symbols do not have fixed meanings. Each of us has our own, unique relationship with life and its different aspects, animals, places and people. So although symbols do often have a cultural meaning and it's useful to be aware of this as we interpret the images, it's also important to remember that the same symbol may convey different messages to different people. For example, take the symbol of *the ocean*. To some, the ocean might be an unpredictable, powerful force beyond our control; to them it may represent our relationship with power. Others might be more aware of the way the ocean shifts and changes its mood; to them, *ocean* may represent feeling or emotion. Others might see its depth, our inability to know or see what lies at the bottom of the ocean; and so to them it may represent the unconscious. None of these interpretations are better than the others. They are simply different.

Listening to our intuition involves fleshing out the substance of each symbol fully until we start to get a sense for what quality (or qualities) it may represent to us. An excellent way to do this is on a mind-map. Place the symbol at the centre, and brainstorm all your associations in the branches and sub-branches. If the symbol has different aspects (a black key; a fast red car; a broken windowpane) create a separate mind-map for each aspect, and then review them together. Ask yourself: *What does that symbol mean to me? How would I describe it to an alien? What associations do I have with it?* Peeling away the layers of meaning, we open into a conversation with our intuition and its wisdom.

Over time, our relationship to our intuition becomes stronger, deeper and more instinctive. We start to understand its language more easily. Perhaps we even become fluent. Yet we never master Intuition; nor should we try. Listening intuitively is not about distilling things down to one truth, or boxing our wisdom into clearly defined answers. Through the eyes of

Intuition, the world retains mystery. It has layers of meaning. It can never fully be defined, categorized or known. It can only be felt, experienced, sensed and received, every day more deeply.

The Gifts of Intuition

The intuitive mind is a sacred gift and the rational mind
is a faithful servant.
We have created a society that honours the servant
and has forgotten the gift.

– ALBERT EINSTEIN

When we do dare to follow our intuition, we are showered with its gifts. Intuition taps into the unconscious, so it brings us into contact with the gifts of the unconscious. These include creativity, insight, power and wisdom, qualities that combine to generate breakthrough ideas, strategies and innovation. Stories throughout history remind us of what's possible when we listen to our intuition – and the dangers that lurk when we don't. We can categorize these possibilities into three areas: creativity, innovation and survival.

Any number of stories highlight the link between Intuition and the creative impulse. The tune for one of the most famous songs of all time, the Beatles' 'Yesterday', came to Paul McCartney in a dream – dreams being one of the most direct and powerful ways of accessing Intuition and the unconscious. It went on to have the most cover versions of any song ever written, according to the Guinness Book of Records, and was performed over seven million times in the 20th century.[28] Another well-known creation, Mary Shelley's *Frankenstein*, came through a waking vision. As guests in the home of Lord Byron, Shelley and the other guests were challenged to tell a ghost story. She recounts the 'birth' of the idea in the introduction to the final work: 'When I placed my head upon my pillow, I did not sleep, nor could I be said to think. My imagination, unbidden, possessed and guided me, gifting the successive images that arose in my mind with a vividness far beyond the usual bound of reverie. I saw – with shut eyes, but acute mental vision – I saw the pale student of unhallowed arts kneeling beside the thing he had put together. I saw the hideous phantasm of a man stretched out, and then, on the working of some powerful engine, show signs of life, and stir with an uneasy, half-vital motion.'[29] This waking vision, which terrified even Shelley, became Frankenstein. Other artists tell similar stories. Robert Louis Stevenson credits the idea for *The Strange Case of Dr. Jekyll and Mr. Hyde* to a dream. Stephen King acknowledges that ideas for his writing often come through dreams.[30] All these stories highlight the link between Intuition and creativity.

Other stories show the power of Intuition to support invention and innovation. Dmitry Mendeleyev, a Russian chemist and inventor, noticed patterns in the chemical properties of different elements to create the Periodic Table – even predicting properties of elements yet to be discovered.[31] Otto Loewi, a German physiologist, won the Nobel Prize for his work on the chemical transmission of nerve impulses. The design for the experiment came to him in a dream as well. It took him a decade to prove his findings to other scientists, yet ultimately the result of his initial (dream-led) experiment became the foundation for his prize-winning theory. Elias Howe received a similar inspiration: he had the idea of creating a machine with a needle that would go through a piece of cloth, but could not figure out exactly how it would work. 'Then one night he dreamt he was taken prisoner by a group of natives. They were dancing around him with spears. As he saw them move around him, he noticed that their spears all had holes near their tips.'[32] Using the insight from the dream, he experimented with a machine that used a needle with a hole at the tip – and in 1845 created the sewing machine.

Scientist James Lovelock writes of this rarely acknowledged link between Intuition and science. 'It is not commonly known, and it is rarely taught in schools that science like art and music is a very intuitive thing. If you ask scientists how they made a discovery, they will tell you it came to me in a flash. And it did. Then they spend at least two years trying to explain it first to themselves and then perhaps ten to forty years trying to explain it to their colleagues. But it comes to you as a flash of intuition and that is the way it happens. Don't be afraid of that. Don't think there is anything wrong about it. When it is written up in the textbooks, it would seem that it was all logical, but that is not how it really happens.'[33]

Sometimes listening to our intuition can be a matter of life and death. President Abraham Lincoln is a famous example of this. Just a few days before he was assassinated, he recounted the following dream to his wife:

> There seemed to be a death-like stillness about me. Then I heard subdued sobs, as if a number of people were weeping. I thought I left my bed and wandered downstairs. There the silence was broken by the same pitiful sobbing, but the mourners were invisible. I went from room to room; no living person was in sight, but the same mournful sounds of distress met me as I passed along. It was light in all the rooms; every object was familiar to me; but where were all the people who were grieving as if their hearts would break?
>
> I was puzzled and alarmed. What could be the meaning of all this? Determined to find the cause of a state of things so mysterious and so shocking, I kept on until I arrived at the East Room, which I entered. There I met with a sickening surprise. Before me was a catafalque, on which rested a corpse wrapped in funeral vestments. Around it were stationed soldiers who were acting as guards; and there was a throng of people, some gazing mournfully upon the corpse, whose face was covered, others weeping pitifully.
>
> 'Who is dead in the White House?' I demanded of one of the soldiers. 'The President,' was his answer; 'he was killed by an

assassin!' Then came a loud burst of grief from the crowd, which awoke me from my dream.[34]

People often ask: *Is Intuition always right?* My answer is: *Yes, through the eyes of the soul.* Intuition will not always take us into the future we envisioned or to the outcome we expected. We may have a really strong intuition to launch a certain product and then see it fail. We may be called towards accepting a job offer, only to find that six months later we are made redundant. We may rearrange everything in our life to move to a less well paid but seemingly more inspiring industry, only to find ourselves disappointed, frustrated and disillusioned with the reality we discover in that new world.

One client I worked with followed his intuition to quit a ten-year career in an impressive multi-national, leave behind the familiarity of his home in England and accept a new job working for an American organization in Bangkok. Leaving an organization in which he was already highly valued and jumping into a new company, a new team and a new country was a risk, but his intuition pulled him towards that risk. As the new role unfolded, his experience was mixed. Living in Bangkok proved rich and interesting, but the job itself was disappointing. On paper, it was a great job – developing a new portfolio of healthy snacks for the developing world in an organization that mostly sold unhealthy products. Yet in reality, he felt that the organization wasn't really committed to this new portfolio. It seemed more of a PR stunt than a true shift of focus. Added to that, he found himself caught up in conflict and power struggles with his boss. After a year, he quit.

Was his intuition right to lead him towards that job? From the point of view of the ego, his experience in Bangkok was a failure: a disappointing, disillusioning and uncomfortable dead-end job. From the point of view of the soul, it was an amazing learning experience that helped him grow into previously unconscious aspects of his inner world. Through that experience he became clear about the importance of integrity, he saw what he did and did not believe in, and he began to uncover his relationship with power and powerlessness. So the move to Bangkok helped him grow and mature, personally and professionally, and through the eyes of the soul it was therefore immensely valuable.

This story may not be of great comfort if you're trying to work out whether to launch a product, accept a job offer, change industries or venture into the enticing and terrifying world of entrepreneurship. Honouring Intuition and following the path of the soul is risky, and it requires courage. Yet it also opens us to vast plains of opportunity that are simply not available if we only follow a linear, step-by-step approach to life. Bringing us into contact with our unconscious, Intuition beckons us towards rewarding (yet risky) possibilities, drawing us ever more fully into life as leaders, organizations and communities.

CASE STUDY | INTUITION AS A PATH TO LEADERSHIP

An Intuitive Path to the Future
Richard Stoppard, Nokia

Richard Stoppard works at Nokia as a director of retail marketing responsible for portfolio and insights. He's 40, smart and ambitious with a larger-than-life personality and a bold, sometimes challenging approach to business. He is also a leader who knows the power of Intuition.

'I guess I always had Intuition,' Richard says. 'But I probably wasn't conscious of using it when I was younger – and it was never really named or encouraged at school or at work.' One of the first times he consciously followed gut feel rather than rational facts was an early career move. At age 26, Richard was working as a buyer at Safeway. Then he was approached by a head-hunter and offered a position with Somerfield, a highly respected retailer: a more senior role, significantly better paid, based outside London, offering a much better quality of life. Looking at the facts, it was a great job – something to enthusiastically say yes to. Yet Richard said no.

'I made the decision in a couple of hours. Actually, truthfully, the inner me had already made the decision. But it took a few hours of quiet time, mulling things over in the bath and zoning out with my thoughts, for the rational mind to catch up with that intuitive decision.' On paper the job was the perfect opportunity, but his gut feel was that it wasn't the right move. He had the intuitive sense: *There must be something better than this around the corner for me.* So he turned the opportunity down. Periodically, in those next few months, his rational mind squirmed and went back over the facts, wondering: *Did I make the right decision?* But there was also a deep trust in the intuitive instinct that stopped Richard from getting too caught up in those doubts. Four months later his intuition was validated. Richard was offered a job at Unilever: well paid, even more senior, in a great location, and this time a role he felt genuinely excited by. 'That role led to great opportunities for me. Meanwhile, a few months later Somerfield made a number of redundancies, which I might well have been part of if I'd accepted their job offer.'

Working in buying, sales and marketing at four different multinational companies, Richard has learned to trust his intuition in wider strategic decisions as well. Sometimes that intuition has shown up uninvited. For example, whilst at Unilever he worked on a consultancy project to redesign sales strategy in Mexico. A survey with internal and external stakeholders clearly showed that the two key priorities were designing trade terms with customers and developing a pricing strategy. Promotional strategy was way down the list, and was therefore not going to be addressed through this project. Yet intuitively Richard sensed that something was missing from this picture and that promotion needed to be included in the conversation even though statistically it seemed less important. So he drew up a model showing the inter-relation between these three different elements of sales and shared it with his boss, who agreed. They took the theory to the wider team and got support for it. This decision, which went against the data, ultimately led to double-digit sales growth.

Other times, Richard has created space for Intuition in a more conscious way. Sometimes he does that alone – exploring an opportunity by sketching out his gut feeling on paper. Or he draws out Intuition with his team by asking a series of open questions: *What's your view of what's going on here? What's your feeling about this situation? Do we think this looks right? Do we think this will work?* Asking these exploratory questions creates a hypothesis, built on a mixture of gut feeling and experience, and starts to paint a picture of what might be going on. Then, and only then, the team turns to the facts and starts to prove or disprove the hypothesis. So there is a sharp focus to their fact-finding, and the information they uncover is set against the larger intuitive picture that has already been sketched out.

For example, arriving in his role at Nokia, Richard noticed that the mobile-phone category was 'a mess'. There was no structure to how products were ordered or laid out in stores, so things were extremely confusing for shoppers. Based on his experience in category management and sales in other organizations, Richard sensed that there was an opportunity to bring order to this chaos. So he brought the team together and made space for their intuitive sense of what was needed. Brainstorming with just a white board and their intuition, the team drew up a hypothesis for how the category might be structured: dividing all mobile-phone products into subcategories and naming each one, agreeing on the colours they would use, how products would be laid out in store and even a couple of options for shelf design. Only then did they turn to the facts and check their hypothesis with shoppers and customers – who loved it.

This story reveals a more general truth: that Intuition lies at the heart of innovation. After all, data is always focused on the past. That's useful, but it's not enough when we want to look towards an unknown future. As Richard points out, 'We can never have rational data for things that haven't happened yet – so when we're looking towards the future, we have to be willing to look beyond and through the facts.' In a brainstorm you don't put together a raft of rational information and expect to find new solutions. You free yourself up from the constraints of functional, fact-based decisions and hope that creativity and imagination will kick in and lead to exciting new ideas. The same is true when trusting your intuition in key strategic decisions. 'Following Intuition is risky – after all, if it goes wrong, there's no way to justify your decision, so you risk being blamed for the failure. But it's also the only way to keep speed and momentum and to find new, breakthrough ways of doing things. I believe all successful organizations have to create room for Intuition – which may mean making room for failure on the way to the greater successes.'

Source: My interview with Richard Stoppard

PRACTICE # 3

Dreams

Dreams are perhaps the most powerful way of accessing the wisdom of the unconscious. They offer us direct insight into our inner world with little or no manipulation from the conscious mind. After all, we don't get to choose our dreams; we don't get to filter out information because we don't like it or because it doesn't fit with our current understanding of who we are. Dreams simply arrive, with or without our permission, and they speak the truth of our unconscious directly to us.

It would be easy write a chapter on how to work with dreams – even a whole book. Since that's not possible here, here are three facts that can immediately change the way you work with your dreams:

- **Every character in the dream is an aspect of your own inner world.** They are the cast of your inner world, the archetypes of the unconscious acting out behind masks of 'mother', 'friend', 'ambitious leader', 'teenage rebel', 'judge or rule-maker', 'policeman or law-enforcer', 'warrior'. This is true for both human and animal characters. Every character in the dream is you.
- **The 'dream ego' (the image of you in the dream) is often mistaken in its assumptions, attitudes and expectations.** Ask yourself: *How might my dream ego be mistaken?*
- **Dreams speak in metaphors – and they mostly reflect the status of your inner world, rather than predicting events in the outer world.** Translate all images and characters through this

metaphorical filter. If you dream you show up at work naked, ask yourself whether you're feeling exposed and vulnerable in your working world. If you dream of being chased, consider where you are running away from a truth, reality or aspect of yourself. If you dream your computer crashes, notice that you are in a radical process of change, or perhaps about to enter one. If you dream you're pregnant, ask yourself what you are ready to give birth to in your life and work.

With that in mind, here's a simple process to help you access the wisdom, insight and creativity of your dreams.

1. Before you go to sleep, **petition** for a dream to give you insight into a particular question or situation. Then **prepare** yourself to receive the dream. Make sure you have a journal and pen or a voice recorder next to your bed. If you have a specific question, write it down at the top of a page in your journal before you go to sleep. As you feel yourself falling towards sleep, bring the question to the edge of your awareness.

2. When you wake up, **capture your dream**, writing it down in as much detail as possible. It's best to do this immediately, before moving too much, while you're still close to the threshold of the dream world. Include what happened, where you were, who else was there and any feelings you had during the dream. It's best to write it in the present tense, for example: *I am walking along a small, dirt track in a foreign country . . .*

3. When you're ready to work with your dream, come back to the story you wrote in your journal. Give it a **title**.

4. On a new page, write down all the **characters** in the dream. Then write four or five words that describe the characteristics of that person – for example, shy, bold, intelligent, needy, emotional, angry, stubborn, materialistic, powerful or weak. If it's someone

from your past, write down your age when you knew him or her.

5. Then go through the dream again and pull out all the **symbols** – for example, *dirt road, gate, ocean, car, house, sofa, vacuum cleaner, passport*. Next to each one, write three or four words that explain what this 'thing' is. It may help to imagine you're describing it to a child or even an alien. This often helps you get to the essence of what it is, and to see its symbolic significance.

6. When you've done that, read the dream back to yourself (out loud if possible). Begin with: **'In my life right now ...'** When you come to a character or symbol, substitute the three or four words you wrote about that particular person or object. So the story of the dream from #2 might read: 'In my life right now, I am walking along a *narrow, under-developed path* in an *unfamiliar part of my inner world where foreign, little-known parts of me belong ...'* Read slowly, and notice any places that trigger an emotional response or an 'aha'. Pause in these places, staying with whatever feelings emerge. Make a note of any key insights or ahas internally and in your journal.

7. Ask yourself: *Is the dream demanding any kind of action or **commitment** in my outer world?* If so, take it.

If you feel like it's a particularly rich dream, you may want to deepen your exploration. There are many ways to do this and below are just a few suggestions:

• You might **act out** the dream – alone, with the support of friends or colleagues or in a dream group.

• If there is a **character** that puzzles, frightens, repulses or intrigues you, try getting to know it (as a part of your inner world). You might 'become' that character: stand the way it would stand, speak the way it would speak, move the way it would move. You can dance as this part of you, you can paint as it, you can write your journal as it, you can go for a nature walk to learn more about it and so on. You could interview it, out loud or by writing in your journal, asking it questions and then allowing the answers to take form. Do whatever feels fun, intriguing, obvious or scary! Notice this character's perspective, how it sees the 'ego' or image of you in the dream, what insight it may offer into the question you asked, what gift it might offer you in your work and life.

- **Paint or draw** your overall experience of the dream (or a particularly powerful scene of the dream) and see what insight or emotion that triggers.

- Ask your unconscious for **another dream**, the following night, to give you more information about a certain aspect of the dream or a character within it.

Remember, with dreams, it's not usually helpful to try to analyse and figure them out to the point where you have absolute clarity about what they are saying and can put them neatly in a box marked 'processed'. Dreams continue to work in us for quite some time, haunting our imagination, helping us see things in our daily lives through new eyes and popping back into our awareness after long periods of absence. Working with dreams is about partnering with the unconscious, making friends with it, listening to the stories it has to tell, and letting those stories shape and guide us in our work and life. Let the dream retain some mystery.

CHAPTER 4

Wildness

Living Beyond the Rules

Ask not what the world needs.
Ask what makes you come alive
… then go do it.
Because what the world needs
Is people who have come alive.

– HOWARD THURMAN –

So listening to our Intuition,
we start to hear our own inner voice.
Yet will we be brave enough to claim this voice as our guide
and allow it to lead us in our journey of transformation?
Will we find the courage to follow our Intuition into our
Wildness – to share our true, authentic self with the world?

Claiming Wildness: My Story

It wasn't exactly with delight that I discovered my gift for working with tarot. To me, tarot readers were old ladies with big rings and purple skirts who muttered dangerous prophecies to naive clients. I, on the other hand, was intelligent, bold, ambitious and professional. In my high-achieving life, 'tarot reader' was not the career path I had mapped out for myself.

For the first years, I kept my newfound intuitive gifts to myself, hidden safely out of sight. I offered the occasional free tarot reading to friends. Over time, I sometimes integrated tarot into sessions with private coaching clients. But I had no intention of making this a formal career, and I certainly wasn't going to bring these spiritual practices to my executive coaching and the business world.

But life had other ideas. It was autumn 2005, almost a year after I'd left Unilever, and I happened to be visiting Unilever's UK office. Walking through reception on my way in, I bumped into a colleague and friend who I'd worked with in Thailand and hadn't seen for years. Walking through reception on the way out, I bumped into him again. 'Funny,' I thought, newly tuned in to Intuition and synchronicity. Taking life's lead, I let go of my afternoon's plans and made time to connect. We spent an hour together, walking by the Thames, watching the swans glide and fight in the afternoon sun. I shared my journey of the last two years; he shared his. At the end of the hour, we set up a formal coaching session.

A few weeks later, I found myself in a glass-walled meeting room at Unilever, tarot cards spread out across the table. An adventurous, open and slightly maverick personality, my client had decided he'd like to experiment with tarot in his coaching session. So there we were, talking about business, using tarot, in the middle of the afternoon at Unilever. At first, I kept watch out of the corner of my eye, conscious of the glass walls and worried about what people might think if they walked past. But slowly, the conversation drew me in, and my self-consciousness dissolved into the connection with my client.

That coaching session opened the door to opportunities that would take my coaching business to the next level. Impressed by his experience, my client recommended me to the organizers of the Marketing Forum, a conference for marketing professionals, held annually on board the cruise ship *Oriana*. At first they were skeptical about including a 'wild card' like me in the program. In fact, they actually said no. But the 'no' didn't feel right to me. I could clearly see myself at that conference. It felt obvious and right. I knew, intuitively, that I would end up there. So I offered the organizer a sample tarot reading free – and finally, courageously, she agreed to include my coaching in the conference agenda.

Then came the true test of my wildness. This was the first business conference I'd been invited to in connection with my new leadership business, Wild Courage, and I desperately wanted to make a good impression. At the same time, I wanted to offer something different, to bring my real gifts to participants. I faced a choice: to expand, take a risk and fling myself fully into the business world; or to tighten up, stay within bounds, and play it safe. In the end, the wild me won. I didn't offer Leadership Coaching; I offered Coaching for the Soul. In the marketing brochure, I didn't talk about leadership style or work challenges; I talked about offering 'a space to explore the deeper questions: *Who am I? Where am I going? What are my gifts? How can I serve? What blocks me?* and other questions of soul'. Then I added a sentence that sent my stomach into free fall: 'For those of you who are feeling bold, we can also explore these questions using tarot.'

These questions are the territory of any powerful coaching session. Yet to bring 'soul' openly into a business conference was unusual; to bring tarot into the conversation was unheard of – except as evening 'entertainment' at a Christmas party. For weeks, my mind whirred with anxiety. Was I humiliating myself? Would people think I was totally mad? Would participants overlook me, as some fluffy, spiritual, woo-woo woman? Could I dare to reveal so much of myself?

Then again, could I dare not to? After all, an exploration of soul *was* what I was offering, and I wanted to be honest about that, not slip it surreptitiously into the conversations disguised in corporate language. Terrified though I was, the idea of offering tarot at a corporate conference also fascinated me. What would it be like to bring this deep, insightful tool into leadership coaching? What might be possible in this meeting of business and soul? Something in me wanted to find out. Some part of me would have it no other way.

So, in September 2006, I stepped on board the grand and magnificent *Oriana* with a suit and tarot cards in my bag. For three days, I came alive in conversations, keynotes, black-tie dinners . . . and, of course, coaching sessions. Sitting in the corner of a bar, looking out through the round windows of the *Oriana*, I laid out tarot cards and watched mature executives dissolve into tears of acknowledgement and appreciation at finally being seen. Every single leader opted to use tarot in their coaching. The sessions were over-subscribed by ten times. They scored an average of 4.9 out of 5 in participants' ratings. And those three days led, directly or indirectly, to 60 per cent of my current work.

So it was with surprise that, three years later, I realized I was rarely using tarot in my coaching sessions. Occasionally, I would reach for the cards, but increasingly I found that I didn't want to. It wasn't that I was shy, nervous or embarrassed about tarot anymore. It was simply that daring to break the rules was no longer what mattered most, and so using tarot or not was irrelevant. The conversation itself had become central, and all that mattered was that I showed up fully: open, spontaneous, receptive and present, ready to connect with the soul of my clients. That was real Wildness; and that was where the real magic began.

The Nature of Wildness

To be nobody but yourself – in a world which is doing its best, night and day, to make you like everybody else – means to fight the hardest battle which any human being can fight, and never stop fighting.

– E E CUMMINGS

We inhabit a world of immense diversity. Our wild earth includes arid desert, rugged mountains, glaciers, grasslands, tropical rainforest and a vast expanse of ocean. Within these diverse landscapes, we find a spectacular array of creatures: an estimated 5 to 30 million species of birds, mammals, insects, fish, flowers, trees, fruits and other forms of life.[35] Each of these has its own unique form, its own way of belonging to life. Each sings its own song, blossoms in its own way, moves according to its own nature. Each plays a key role in its ecosystem, dancing with life in its own unique way. Each embodies Wildness.

Somehow we understand and accept Wildness in the natural world. According to the *Oxford English Dictionary*, in the animal world, *wild* is 'living in a state of nature; not tame, not domesticated'. For a plant or flower, it is 'growing in a state of nature; not cultivated'. Yet when we apply Wildness to the human world, it takes on a wholly different character. The neutral definition, 'living in a state of nature', gives way to judgmental and defended definitions. Here are just some of the words the *Oxford English Dictionary* uses to define *wild* in the human world, based on the ways it's been used in Western literature (my italics):

* Uncivilized, *savage*; uncultured, *rude*; not accepting, or resisting, the constituted government; rebellious.
* Resisting control or restraint, unruly, restive; flighty, thoughtless; *reckless, careless*.

* Not submitting to moral control; taking one's own way in defiance of moral obligation or authority; unruly, insubordinate; *wayward, self-willed.*

* Giving way to sexual passion; also, more widely, *licentious, dissolute, loose.*

* Fierce, savage, ferocious; furious, *violent, destructive, cruel.*

* Not having control of one's mental faculties; *demented,* out of one's wits; distracted; . . . extremely *foolish* or unreasonable; holding absurd or fantastic views.

* Of undertakings, actions, notions, statements, etc.: . . . *going to extremes of extravagance or absurdity;* fantastically unreasonable.

* Not under, or not submitting to, control or restraint; taking, or disposed to take, one's own way; uncontrolled; . . . going at one's own will; unconfined, unrestricted.[36]

These definitions show how much Wildness is rejected and feared in our 'civilized' modern societies. Of the eight definitions shared above, only the last is relatively neutral in its interpretation of the word. The others are almost laughable in their disdain and judgment of this word *wild.* It's clear that Wildness is firmly embedded in our shadow, its gifts and qualities largely lost to us as leaders.

What does it really mean to be 'wild'? And what gifts does it bring? Over a hundred years ago, Nietzsche explored these questions through a story in *Thus Spake Zarathustra.* Nietzsche calls it 'On the Three Metamorphoses'. I prefer to call it 'The Camel, the Lion and the Child'. Here it is, retold in my words with some poetic licence.

Once upon a time, long ago and far away, there lived a camel, and the camel's name was Carlos. Bright-eyed and well-groomed, Carlos was a very good camel. He was kind, polite, strong, hard-working, helpful and reliable. All the other camels liked him. 'Carlos, oh yes, he is a very good camel,' they said. And Carlos felt proud.

The years passed and Carlos started to get tired. Trying to be good was exhausting. And although he was popular and successful, somehow his life lacked joy. Weighed down with expectations and obligations, he started to feel heavy and burdened. His eyes became dull and his fur rough. Looking up at the twinkling stars one night, Carlos was suddenly flooded with sadness. 'Surely there is more to life than this?' he thought.

And so he set out into the desert, alone, in search of his joy. For many days and many nights, Carlos journeyed through the dry sands of the desert. The days were long and lonely. Many times, he thought to turn back. But each time, his heart propelled him forwards with its longing.

One day, far from home, Carlos woke to a thundering roar. Jumping to his feet, he found himself face to face with a huge, scaly golden dragon. Carlos held his breath, waiting to die. But then, in the reflection of the dragon's beady eye, he caught sight of a fierce golden lion. And as flames leapt from the dragon's mouth, Carlos, now a Lion, roared. Swiping his large claws, he began to fight for his life.

For three days and three nights, Carlos the Lion battled with the dragon, Thou Shalt. Over and over he pounced, tearing the scales from the dragon's body, each scale a golden 'thou shalt'. As he ripped each scale from the dragon's body, Carlos recognized it as a rule he'd adopted as a Camel. 'No,' he roared, again and again, as he tore these rules from the dragon's body. 'I will, I will,' his cry for freedom echoed across the empty desert. Finally, the battle was over. Carlos was victorious; the dragon lay lifeless in the sand.

Exhausted from the fight, Carlos dropped to the ground. Looking down at his paws, he found himself amazed. His lion's claws had become small, soft hands and feet. Carlos the Lion had become a child. And so it was that Carlos the Child returned home, skipping across the desert, his heart filled with joy. Full of life, radiant, graceful and free, he made his way back to his tribe, his sacred 'Yes' echoing across the vibrant and listening desert.

As Nietzsche's story reminds us, Wildness has two faces: a sacred *no* and a sacred *yes*. As the Lion, we must learn to say no. That means challenging the status quo, breaking the rules, stepping outside conventions and forging our own authentic path into the world. Yet sometimes we can get stuck in the Lion phase, attached to our identity of Rebel or Maverick. We fight against the system, and we think that this makes us free. Yet we are still defining ourselves on its terms. So long as we are fighting the rules, we are still bound up in them. So long as we are struggling against anything, we are not fully free. As the story reminds us, the Lion is only an interim stage in the journey to Wildness.

The ultimate expression of Wildness is not the Lion but the Child. This is a surprising twist to the story. After all, we might expect to emerge from our battle with the dragon as a wise sage or a powerful leader. Yet we don't. We emerge as a Child: innocent, natural, spontaneous, vulnerable and pure. As the Child, we learn to say yes: to do what we love, follow our bliss, lean towards the experiences, people and places that bring us alive. Moved by wonder, we follow our curiosity and our joy, from moment to moment, with no plans and strategies. We turn inwards and follow our true nature, without complicating or rationalizing it. Beyond the rules and the fighting, we enter into a natural, simple and spontaneous relationship with ourselves, each other and life. This is the ultimate expression of Wildness.

As the Child, we continue to fulfill responsibilities in the world – to a team, a family, a mission. Yet there is a sense of spaciousness within our responsibilities, rather than a sense of sacrifice. We commit freely, a sacred 'yes', and we allow that 'yes' to re-express itself in every moment, rather than holding on to rigid definitions of who we are and who we are not. That means making space for our whole self – for all the different energies of our soul – and letting the archetypes of our inner world dance and shift and re-express themselves in each moment. We don't hold on to identities that *seem* free or wild. We don't *try* to be anything. We simply live, moment to moment, fully present with ourselves and the world.

Reclaiming Wildness

Re-examine all you have been told . . .
Dismiss what insults your Soul.

– WALT WHITMAN

Why do we live, like the Camel, so heavily burdened with other people's rules? Usually because at some deep level we believe that conforming to these rules and expectations is the way to be loved and accepted. Growing up, we are rewarded for certain behaviours and scolded or punished for others; we become popular for some personality traits and unpopular because of others. We learn pretty quickly: *When I'm too loud/quiet, I get in trouble; when I am angry/sad, people don't like me; being clever/average makes me popular; when I look different/geeky, I get teased.* Parents, teachers and society flood us with messages, both formal and subtle, about who we should be and who we should not be. In our attempt to be loved, we adapt, shaving off parts of our wild nature to fit in and belong. This is a clever strategy, and in some cases it's actually the only way to survive. From the point of view of the Camel, either we mould ourselves into what others want us to be or we face being ostracized, rejected, outcast, unloved and unwanted. Given that choice, little wonder that we tame our wild natures to fit in.

It's not just our parents and peers who influence us in this way. The system itself is designed to shape us into 'useful', productive parts of the social machinery. In the early 20th century, Elwood Cubberly, Dean of Education at Stanford University, proclaimed that schools should be factories 'in which raw products (children) are to be shaped and formed into finished products . . . manufactured like nails, with the specifications set by industry'.[37] We have hopefully come some way from these archaic and rigid views of education. Yet a hundred years later, echoes of his opinion still resonate. Learning 'useful' skills that set us up for well-paid careers is heavily favoured. Even now, formal education is less about developing, supporting and drawing out our wild natures, and more about shaping and moulding us to fit into existing social and economic systems.

This is not only true of our educational systems; it's also true of organizational life. There too, we are assessed and measured against a set of criteria that lay out who we should be. Performance reviews are littered with comments that remind us we are too emotional, too sensitive, too insensitive, too aggressive, too timid, too this, too that. As we strive to progress through our working lives, we learn to tame and shape ourselves into more 'useful' leaders and managers who better fit the criteria required by our team or organization.

Many successful people speak of this pressure to become something other than their true selves. Early in her career, whilst she was working as a newsreader, the TV station asked Oprah Winfrey to change her name to Suzie. They felt Suzie was a friendlier name and easier to remember. Oprah said no.[38] J K Rowling, multi-millionaire author of the Harry Potter books and possibly one of the most imaginative people on the planet, was discouraged from studying English literature at university because her parents felt that a vocational degree would be more useful. As she says: 'I was convinced that the only thing I wanted to do, ever, was to write novels. However, my parents, both of whom came from impoverished backgrounds and neither of whom had been to college, took the view that my overactive imagination was an amusing personal quirk that would never pay a mortgage or secure a pension.' So, at the age of 21, Rowling found herself 'striking an uneasy balance between the ambition I had for myself and what those closest to me expected of me'. It took spectacular 'failure', in the eyes of the world, for Rowling to finally connect back to her essential nature. Jobless, a single parent and 'as poor as it's possible to be in modern Britain', Rowling hit rock bottom. With nowhere else to go, she finally stepped into her Wildness, honouring her gifts and passions and becoming a writer. With that move, a different kind of success became possible: one that was not only financially rewarding, but also emotionally and spiritually rewarding, for herself and her readers.[39]

Living by other people's rules can work for some time. Yet at some point these rules start to feel too small. They begin to suffocate us. We start to sense that our true gifts are lost, somewhere within, whilst a polite, mildly robotic person is moving through our work and life. We may notch up huge amounts of external success, but it doesn't fulfill us. We may seem popular, but we still don't feel loved. Disconnected from our true nature, no amount of money, fame or recognition can fill us up. At some level, we're aware that people are not actually loving *us*, they are loving an image of us that we've created. Our true self still lies within, unseen and unaccepted. Conforming in order to be loved is a game rigged for failure!

Realizing this, we are propelled into a journey to Wildness, and we set out to fight for our freedom. Alone in the desert of our lives, we encounter the dragon, Thou Shalt, with his golden scales of inherited rules and rigid understandings of 'value'. In our lives, those rules can be subtle or obvious, general or specific. They might include: 'thou shalt' *put your kids through private school; make lots of money; reject money; work in a 9-to-5 job; never work in a 9-to-5 job; avoid risk; speak quietly; be noticed; do what is asked of you; agree with your boss; avoid confrontation; challenge everything; dress conservatively; dress alternatively.*

As the Lion, our task is to see these rules – and to move beyond them. Fierce, predatory, passionate, we tear away the rules. We say no to bosses, peers, teachers, parents and partners. Equally challenging, we say no to the internal rule-maker. Saying no may be frightening, and it may make us unpopular at times. It may be uncomfortable, leaving us feeling selfish, mean or rude. Yet the story reminds us it is a sacred no. It allows us to hold on to our integrity, to live by our own values, and to set boundaries that take care of our deeper needs. Whistle-blowers at Enron and other less-than-honest organizations are extreme examples of Lion leaders. Clients I've worked with have had their own versions of 'no': *no, I am not willing to work until 2am; no, I don't believe we can achieve those targets; no, I'm not willing to play this political game; no, I don't want to take a job in China; no, I cannot ignore this bullying; no, I don't believe we should compromise on the quality of this product.*

Even a small 'no' can have a dramatic impact. Take, for example, a lawyer I worked with. Newly qualified, she found herself wondering whether the law was really the right environment for her. She was passionate about justice, and she found aspects of her work deeply rewarding. The real problem was much simpler: she was exhausted. Working until midnight or 2am on a regular basis did not work for her. She was too sensitive. She needed time alone, space, down time, rest. Leaning into the journey of Wildness, she discovered that she simply needed to set better boundaries at work. So she committed to leave by 8pm every night, choosing projects and clients that allowed that. At the same time, she stopped hiding her sensitivity and brought it openly into the workplace, naming it in her performance review as both a strength and a limitation. As she reset her working habits, she realized she did not need to change jobs or industries (for the time being). She simply needed to allow herself to bring her wild self to work and to honour her own needs within the workplace.

The choices we've made in the past are rarely a complete mistake, even when we have been influenced by external expectations and obligations. So the challenge as a Lion leader is to embrace these choices – and grow beyond them. Fighting the dragon, we realize that each rule has served in its own quirky and peculiar way. The pressure to pursue a more vocational career, instead of the English degree she wanted, led J K Rowling to study classics and Greek mythology as a compromise – echoes of which resonate throughout her writing. The pressure I felt to be 'successful' led me into business and marketing – which was invaluable experience when it came to setting up Wild Courage. Fighting the dragon is not just about throwing away old, outdated rules. It also involves a fierce honouring of the role each rule played. Only when we honour it can we really let it go, and move beyond it, and step fully into the freedom of the Child leader within.

At this stage in human development, it's hard to imagine how society or organizations would function if more of us were leading as the Child. We are so deeply conditioned to conform that this kind of reality feels utopian and frankly unrealistic. Yet some visionary and courageous organizations are experimenting with moving beyond rules. Just Giving (First Giving in the USA), a website that makes charitable donations quick and easy, is one example of this. At Just Giving, there is no organizational chart; teams form and dissolve for specific projects, with some more permanent than others. Even more radical, there are no rules on holidays or expenses, and people set their own salaries. 'Rules breed mediocrity, not excellence,' CEO Zarine Kharas believes. Creating a culture without rules shifts the role of employees from 'people who follow the rules' to 'people looking for better ways of doing things', generating an innovative and challenging environment. Just Giving is still a tough and rigorous environment. Yet the organizational culture is based on the belief that people come to work to do the right thing. This is the glue, not a set of rules that employees are forced to follow blindly. Eliminating rules, Just Giving claims the freedom of the Child and centres itself on something much more powerful than rules: trust.[40]

So how do we discover our own childlike wildness, our sacred yes? From the journeys I've witnessed, and the stories I've heard, it seems we follow one central question: *What brings me alive?* Within this question are three strands, which help us move more deeply into our wildness.

1. What are my gifts?

2. What brings me joy?

3. What do I serve? (Where do my gifts and joy meet the needs of the world?)

As we focus on these questions, we are drawn towards our essence – our soul. As we claim our Wildness, our lives and work take on greater meaning and purpose. Our relationship with work changes from survival (earning money) to aliveness (a way of bringing our true selves into the world). Our work becomes a way in which we come alive – a sacred yes.

Making the move into Wildness and claiming our sacred work can be terrifying. It's one thing to fail at something we don't love or believe in. If it doesn't work out, we can always explain it by reminding ourselves we weren't that committed to it in the first place. And, anyway, we haven't played our last card – we still have a dream, which can comfort and support us in difficult times. Yet when we step into our vocation and commit to it, we play our last card. We have no more get-out clauses. If we fail at this, then what? We have no more dreams to fall back on. So we risk not only failing, but also losing the comfort and hope held in our unlived dream. Hardly surprising, then, that we find a million excuses to avoid making the move into Wildness. *Now's not the right time. I'm not that talented. How would I pay the mortgage? I don't really want it,* and various other intricate defences that prevent us from stepping into our wildness and claiming our sacred work.

If you do find yourself paralysed on the edge of change, psychologically downsizing and pulling away from living wildly, it may help to refocus on the sacredness of what you are intending to do. Wildness is one of the most precious gifts you have to offer life. Become the Hollow Bone. Get out of your own way and let life live through you. Yes, of course, there are challenges to be overcome and practicalities to be attended to. Just don't let your fear hold you back. Moving towards Wildness is a courageous move, no doubt about it. And aren't its gifts worth that risk?

The Gifts of Wildness

Do not go where the path may lead.
Go instead where there is no path,
and leave a trail.

– RALPH WALDO EMERSON

Reclaiming our wildness brings freedom and joy, which radically shifts our relationship with work. Connected to our true nature, our work is not a burden but a gift that brings us alive. We work hard – but it's *our* work. It feeds us just as much as we feed it. That's not to say that we love every minute of it, or that we never find it dull, tedious, frustrating or burdensome. Some days we would rather stay in bed. Yet deep inside, we feel bonded with our work in a powerful and intimate way. Our commitment to it goes beyond the surface, with its changing moods. Even on a bad day, we know: *This is my work; this is my life; this is the way my soul belongs in the world.* Walking away from it is not an option; it would mean walking away from your self. And as a Child leader, that is no longer possible.

Although it brings great personal reward, Wildness is not just a selfish act; it is our gift to life. In his bestselling business book *Good to Great*, Jim Collins shows that great organizations and individuals are driven by three questions:

1. What are you deeply passionate about?

2. What could you be best in the world at?

3. What drives your economic engine?[41]

Interestingly, these three questions echo the soul-driven questions that guide us into Wildness. So living wildly by following our passion, discovering our gifts, and offering them in service to others is not just a nice thing to do. It's also how we contribute to our communities and organizations. Perhaps the path to soul may also be the path to success.

Oprah's story brings this to life. At the age of 22, Oprah was working as a newsreader on the 6 o'clock news in Baltimore. Objectively it was a great job, yet in reality it didn't actually suit her. As she reported on people's tragedies, every instinct told her to step in, to help, to lend a hand. Yet her job description told her to stand on the sidelines and give an objective report. After eight months, Oprah lost that job because she was 'too emotional', and she found herself hosting a talk show. She says, 'The moment I sat down on that show . . . I felt like I'd come home. I realized that TV could be more than just a playground, but a platform for service, for helping other people lift their lives.' In the right job, Oprah's natural instinct to emotionally engage and support people was not a problem – it was a gift. Whereas as a newsreader she was always striving to be something or someone (else), this role felt natural – 'like breathing'.[42] Claiming her wild nature brought purpose and meaning to her work. In time, it also brought compassion, comfort, support and love to millions of other people. Her story reminds us that living wildly is not selfish; it is a sacred act, deeply tied to service.

Reclaiming Wildness also opens the way for creativity and innovation. *Innovate* comes from the Latin *in* + *novare*, and literally means 'to make new'. In the words of the OED, it is 'to make changes in something established'. It is Wildness that allows us to create these changes, helping us to break free of the rules, conventions and traditions of our team, industry or institution – or even of society as a whole. Without a willingness to break the rules, we would never discover new territories, new opportunities or new ways of being in the world. Without the courage to become the Lion, we stagnate and so do our organizations, institutions and societies.

Our challenge with innovation is to find the right degree of Wildness. Once again, Brian Swimme's discussion on the powers of the universe offers an interesting perspective on this.[43] Taking a community of squirrels as an example, he explains how the genetic coding of the squirrel population remembers and records qualities that have assisted life in previous generations, then hands these qualities down from generation to generation through the squirrels' DNA. Then the context changes: the squirrels move up the mountainside. Here the air has less oxygen, and this puts stress on the bodies of the squirrels. Over time, the DNA of the squirrel population adapts. It changes to incorporate the new value – an ability to absorb oxygen more easily.

Establishing the right degree of mutation is a delicate issue. So life sets up a series of tests to determine whether the various genetic mutations are acceptable and useful. The first test is in the womb, where the mother's body will abort the baby if it deviates too much from the existing system. The second test comes later, as the young squirrel seeks to find a mate and reproduce. If it's too different, it will be rejected by the community and won't be able to find a mate. If the new quality fails either of these tests, the mutation won't be passed on. However, if it passes the tests, the squirrel will reproduce. Over time, because of the laws of natural selection, the genetically advanced squirrels will have more babies. In this way, the modification will spread through the population, eventually becoming the norm for all squirrels.

The same process of evolution and innovation applies in the context of brands, organizations and institutions. Here, too, the challenge is to find the right degree of Wildness. Mihaly Csikszentmihalyi, best-selling author of *Flow* and world-renowned expert in creativity, highlights this need for just the right level of novelty. He argues that innovation usually fails for one of three reasons.

1. It fails because management is too set in its ways to spot good ideas or to imagine the possibilities of breakthrough innovations.

2. It fails because management becomes obsessed with novelty, with no ability to judge and discriminate.

3. It fails because management doesn't have the energy and courage to push good ideas into the mainstream.[44]

In other words, innovation fails when it gets the balance of Wildness wrong. Successful innovation holds the middle ground between tradition and novelty. It acknowledges and builds on the rules and conventions of the establishment, and it is also willing to break these rules.

We can see this process of evolution and innovation as a bell curve. At the centre of the bell curve we have the mainstream values. On the left, at the trailing end of the bell curve, are values and behaviours that have become outdated and are being phased out. On the right, at the emerging edge of the bell curve, are novel and innovative values and behaviours. As with genetic innovation, not all novelties will survive. Some may be too radical for their time. Others may be novel but fail to serve a genuine need. Innovations and changes that do add value, giving people something they genuinely need, usually take hold. Gradually, more and more people move towards them. As these new values, perspectives and qualities become accepted and adopted by the mainstream, the bell curve gradually shifts towards the right and a new benchmark is established. This is the process of progress and evolution.

The diagram (right) highlights a few things about the nature of innovating. First, it helps show why innovative companies get bought out. Founders often get a lot of criticism for selling their companies. When Ben & Jerry's was sold to Unilever, Green & Black's to Cadbury, and Innocent to Coca-Cola, press coverage and popular opinion spoke of 'selling out'. Yet this judgment is a little harsh. As the ideas become more mainstream, it makes sense, in a way, for a more mainstream company to take them over. Absorbing innovative, rule-breaking organizations into the mainstream while still holding on to their essence and values is, of course, a challenge. But it's also a natural movement. Perhaps the founders are more at home, and their gifts better used, at the edge of the bell curve, looking forwards to the next innovations, rather than sliding into the mainstream with their now-mainstream brands? Perhaps we should be a little less quick to call them 'greedy' or 'sell outs', and accept that letting go of their creations may

The Bell Curve of Innovation

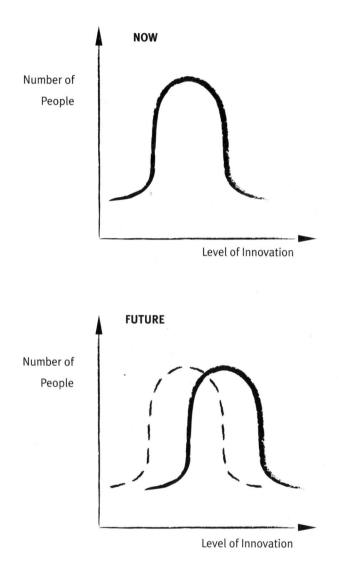

be actually an inevitable expression of their wildness and their need to live and innovate at the edge?

The bell curve highlights another feature of innovating: that it may be a lonely experience. As the Lion, we venture into the wilderness, leaving everything and everyone we know behind. We go alone. The bell curve of innovation shows why: relatively few people inhabit the edges of innovation. As we become more pioneering, we find fewer and fewer people who share our views and values. Loneliness is an inevitable part of living at the edge, embodying new, innovative qualities and ways of being in the world. As Swimme says, 'Those people that feel most wounded and most cut off in this moment (of history) are the ones who have the greatest capacity for providing what is needed (now). Because they are the ones who are actually already feeling the way in which the universe has made a judgment on the Cenozoic era: it's over!'[45] Leaning towards the edge of the bell curve, we make space for our emerging future. We draw it into our current reality. And so we bring new life to our selves as well as to our organizations, institutions and communities. If you are one of the lonely pioneers, perhaps knowing this may comfort you.

CASE STUDY   WILDNESS AS A PATH TO LEADERSHIP

The Journey to Wildness

Richard Reed, Founder of Innocent

Innocent is a UK-based organization selling fresh fruit smoothies, drinks and (more recently) healthy ready meals. Launched in 1998 by three friends, Richard Reed, Adam Balon and Jon Wright, Innocent is now a well-loved company with over £100 million annual turnover. It is also readily associated with a move towards ethical, sustainable business.

The creation of Innocent was a journey into Wildness. It began conventionally enough: three Cambridge graduates working in advertising and management consulting, heading along a mainstream path to 'success'. Then, four years into their conventional careers, Richard, Adam and Jon found themselves on a ski trip in Europe. There, they set themselves a challenge: to come up with an idea for a new business by the end of the holiday. That idea was Innocent: a nutritional, tasty, all-natural, 'innocent' smoothie.

Coming home, the three began trying out recipes on their friends. Six months later, they spent £500 on fruit and sold their smoothies at a UK music festival. In front of their stand, they put up a big sign saying, 'Do you think we should give up our jobs to make these smoothies?' They put out a bin marked YES and a bin marked NO and asked people to put their empty bottles in one bin or the other. At the end of the weekend the YES bin was full. The next day they resigned from their jobs.

Letting go of secure income and prestigious jobs was their first 'sacred no', and it opened the way for their journey into Wildness. Securing funding for their idea was the next challenge. Innocent applied to banks and venture capitalist firms for backing. None of these mainstream organizations were willing to support them. Still, the founders continued to believe in their idea, so in an act of determination and courage, they sent an e-mail to everyone in their address books. The subject line of the e-mail was: 'Does anyone know anyone rich?' Through that last desperate effort, they found a private investor and Innocent was born.

Co-founder and CEO Richard Reed tells the story like this: 'Starting up, everyone said it wouldn't work. No one would lend us any money. They said that the idea to use real fruit rather than concentrates was stupid, that we should put preservatives in to extend shelf life, that we should bulk it out with cheap ingredients so we could make more profit. And we said: "That's not what we do." We went to see every single major manufacturer in the UK and they all said the same thing: "You don't understand the industry, that's how you need to do it." And we said, "Look, you don't understand. We've only got one business idea and that's called Innocent; to keep our drinks completely natural, the way you make them at home."'

Staying true to their original idea involved ferocious Wildness. They could have diluted the concept. They could have bought into conventional wisdom and followed the rules of the drinks market at that time. They didn't. They held on to their vision. They focused their energy on developing a product they believed in. When they encountered resistance from the existing system, they simply kept saying: *This is who we are. This is what we do. This is what we believe.* This is a classic example of the simplicity and authenticity of Child leadership.

In time, Innocent's wildness challenged more than just the conventions of the category; it challenged the whole ethos of business. From the outset, their idea was not just to create a healthy nutritional drink in a market dominated by sugary, carbonated products with no nutritional value. Their vision was also to leave things a little better than they found them, at every level – for the people who bought their drinks and for employees, suppliers, communities and the planet itself. That meant offering a nutritious drink, and it also meant working with local charities, using green electricity and putting pressure on their suppliers to do the same, pioneering recyclable plastic bottles, working closely with farmers and communities to ensure the fruit was grown sustainably, and so on. For the founders of Innocent, following their passion involved finding new ways of doing business, across the board.

Innocent's purpose is anchored in a deep sense of service. Yes, they've been financially successful, and yes, that's important. But from the point of view of Wildness, the passion, commitment and social change that Innocent has generated is just as important as the financial return. It may even be the reason for that financial return. As Richard Reed explains: 'I for one don't ever want to downplay financial stuff. You've got to make money, you've got to grow. And we will not achieve our long-term aims if we screw it up financially. But if we really think our long-term aim is purely financial then I'd walk out tomorrow because, you know what, it's just not that interesting. The money is a really cool side benefit of doing something really important – but it's not important in itself. Our hope with Innocent is that we might, we might be able to become an example to show that there is a slightly more evolved form of capitalism where you can chase profit and growth and all those things and serve a wider social and environmental picture.'

Innocent is a powerful example of how wild, courageous leaders can create a soulful brand – and how that soulful brand can create significant change in the world. It will be interesting to track how Innocent is affected by its partial buy-out by Coca-Cola in 2009 and 2010. Will Innocent's leaders be able to stay authentic and wild under this new ownership? Will innovation still be able to thrive amid the systems and processes of a large multinational? Will the soul of the organization survive? Only time will tell. Yet even if it doesn't, Innocent's Wildness has already left its mark – on both the drinks category and the wider business world.

CASE STUDY   WILDNESS AS A PATH TO LEADERSHIP

Leading with Your Whole Self

Sheryl O'Loughlin, (Former) CEO of Clif Bar

Sheryl O'Loughlin's career also began conventionally. Graduating from the University of Michigan with a business degree, she worked in marketing for several multinational organizations. There, like all Camel leaders, she left her wild self at the door each morning and focused on being what the environment asked her to be. 'At work, I was a cooler, more robotic version of myself. I went through the motions – looking at the numbers, cranking out new flavors, knowing my place. I left my love of adventure, debate and collaboration and my true passions for the outdoors and family at home.'

In 1997, a series of synchronicities opened Sheryl's path to Wildness. On a run, a buddy introduced her to her first Clif Bar, and she was immediately inspired by the concept behind it. A few days later she was looking through an alumni newsletter and found an ad to start a brand management team at Clif Bar. Jumping at the chance, Sheryl flew from Chicago to Berkeley to interview. 'I walked through the doors of the office and onto another planet. The office was colourful, dogs were running around; people were laughing and wearing casual clothes. The place was alive. I felt good there.' Sheryl only had one interview that day, and it was with Gary Erickson, Clif Bar's founder and owner. Throughout that interview, Gary's three-year-old daughter, Lydia, sat on his knee. Gary asked about Sheryl's professional experience, and also about her values and what made her feel joyful. 'Between questions and answers, Lydia playfully whispered in his ear. I had never seen such a whole and integrated person at work. Sitting at his desk, Gary was not only the founder and owner of the company, he was also a loving father, a husband, an athlete, a baker, an inventor, and a happy guy. It was all there, and it was all visible. It was fantastic.'

Sheryl took the job, and started working at Clif Bar. Once there, her journey into Wildness deepened. 'I saw that, like Gary, people at Clif Bar brought their whole selves to work. They eagerly shared their passions and frustrations, and they willingly spoke of their fears and their hopes. He tore away the image that to be good, you had to look or act a certain way. As I engaged with Gary and the other folks at Clif Bar, I finally felt like myself at work. I was starting to become whole again.'

Leading with Wildness opened the way for innovation. In her early days at Clif Bar, despite the camaraderie she felt with colleagues, Sheryl felt detached from the product. Clif Bar was an essentially male creation. Though Sheryl ate them during hardcore rides, she didn't devour them because they had too many calories and, although they tasted good, they were not decadent. Given the freedom to express that was part of the culture at Clif Bar, Sheryl shared her experience. Other women in the company agreed. So, breaking the conventions of the category, they set out to develop a nutrition bar specifically for women. The LUNA bar had fewer calories and featured female-specific nutrients, like folic acid and calcium. 'It was decadent and delicious, which wasn't traditional for an energy bar but was totally appropriate for a nutritious treat. The wrapper depicted women dancing under the moon, a universe away from Clif Bar's masculine mountain climber and (competitor) Power Bar's macho packaging. The story on the back talked about joy, sisterhood and our giving back to the Breast Cancer Fund.'

Launching LUNA required courage and conviction. As with many breakthrough innovations, the mainstream doubted its potential. 'Lots of people blasted our Great Idea. So-called expert marketing consultants told us that LUNA would never take off, and even our internal salespeople were worried. One sales guy told me that there was no way he could sell a "bar for chicks." Criticism was relentless for a while, and those of us who really believed in this product were sweating it.' Still, they stood by their idea. LUNA Bar launched in April 1999 with minimal marketing support. Its creators had no idea of its value – only some cheap online research that confirmed the concept had merit. To their surprise, LUNA became a $10 million business in one year, and was profitable from the word go. Within three years, it became the number one energy bar in the market, a $70 million business, surpassing even the original Clif Bar's revenue.

Yet Wildness can be hard to hold on to. Several years later, in 2004, the low-carb craze swept through the USA, slicing $20 million (30 per cent) off LUNA's revenue. In response, LUNA rushed to launch a low-carb bar, fast. In the rush, they compromised their core strengths and values, using artificial ingredients and sacrificing their high standards of taste. It didn't work. People hated LUNA Glow. Meanwhile, the bottom fell out of the low-carb market. Clif Bar pulled LUNA Glow after six months.

LUNA Glow failed because it lost touch with its essence and fell back into following other people's rules. It was a mistake that cost half a million dollars and damaged the brand's credibility with LUNA lovers, retailers and employees. Ultimately, though, it encouraged LUNA to re-centre in Wildness. As Sheryl puts it: 'Innovation is born from the shit that goes wrong. After LUNA Glow's failure, we spent a lot of time in groups defining what was important in our products, to our consumers and to us. It defined the parameters for our innovation, and this made the target easier to hit. Instead of retreating into an innovation freeze, we grew our portfolio from four brands in 2004 to sixteen in 2007: a threefold increase.' Failure pointed Clif Bar and LUNA back onto the path of Wildness.

Source: My interviews with Richard Reed and Sheryl O'Loughlin; Laura Cummings, 'Just an Innocent Business?', BBC News, 9 July 2003, http://news.bbc.co.uk/1/hi/business/3014477.stm; transcript of Sheryl O'Loughlin's speech to the Mars leadership team.

PRACTICE # 4

Story

Story is one of the oldest forms of sharing and discovering our experience of being human. Myths and fairy tales have travelled through many thousands of years, sometimes verbally, sometimes in pictures on cave walls or clay tablets, more recently in written form. Across time, human beings have used story as a way of passing down teachings and insights from generation to generation.

Traditional stories are full of colourful characters. They represent the archetypes of our unconscious: wicked witch, ugly stepsister, prince or princess, naive Red Riding Hood, trickster wolf, power-hungry ruler, noble hero and heroine. The story we explored in chapter 4 presented three such archetypes: Camel, Lion and Child. These characters are the cast of our inner world. Engaging with them through journaling, art, drama or imagination, we bring unconscious parts of our selves into our awareness so that we can access their gifts and work consciously with their more challenging traits.

Writing or telling our personal stories can also bring perspective to the challenges and dynamics of our work and lives. When we explore our lives through story, we bypass the rational mind and tap into the intuitive function. Writing the fairy tale of our life, from birth to the present moment (and beyond), can help us see the patterns at play in the bigger picture of our life and offer insight into the choices and challenges of the present moment. Speaking our story out loud, even with no audience, can sometimes help us shift perspective or find an emotional release in an intense situation. When we go one step further, and share these stories with others, we co-create a tapestry of human experience from which we can connect, learn and grow.

Story does not have to be told in words – we can also use images. We don't need to be 'good' artists to use this approach; finger paints, play dough and pictures from magazines are all equally effective. It's not about producing a masterpiece for our fridge; it's about using imagery to explore the patterns of our unconscious.

Here are some guidelines on how to write or artistically express your story.

1. Before you begin, choose the medium you'd like to work with and **gather the necessary materials** – a journal; finger paints and paper; card, magazines, scissors and glue. Decide how long you will spend on the activity.

2. When you're ready to begin, pause and centre, preparing to step into unfamiliar parts of your inner world. Get clear on your **intention or question**. It might be something general, for example, *I want to understand the deeper patterns of my life*. It might be to explore your relationship with one of the qualities in this book. Or it might be to get insight into a particular project, situation or decision. When your intention is clear, open the space by lighting a candle or choosing music that helps you drop into the creative flow.

3. Holding your question in your awareness, **begin the creative process**. If you're drawing or painting, let your hand(s) move without thinking too hard. If you're doing a collage, let yourself be drawn to pictures and images, even if you're not quite sure why. If you're writing a story, let the words form on the page without thought or judgment – just as in the practice of Journaling. Let the story emerge. You may like to experiment with using your non-dominant hand to support you in bypassing the rational mind.

4. When you feel the story is complete, stop. Re-centre. Thank your unconscious for playing! Then **close the activity** by blowing out

the candle, turning off the music and intentionally moving back into your everyday state of consciousness.

5. Come back to your story after a short break and see what you notice. **Look with fresh eyes,** as though it were someone else's work of art. What do the images and characters of the story tell you about the person who created it? What feelings does it trigger? What insight does it offer into your challenge or question? You may like to journal around these questions. Pay particular attention to anything that surprises you or stirs up strong emotion.

6. If you feel you want to go deeper, you may like to **share your story.** That might be with another human being, or with an animal or place in the natural world that you feel connected to. Experiment with how you tell your story. Maybe you could tell it as a fairytale, or in the third person or as a poem or movement. Notice what you share as well as what you leave out. Notice how you feel when you're telling your story – and how you feel afterwards. Notice too what happens around you as you tell your story.

7. Does the experience of creating or sharing your story prompt any **commitments** or actions? If so, take them.

CHAPTER 5

Vulnerability

Exposing and Engaging Soul

When we were children, we used to think
that when we were grown up we would no longer be vulnerable.
But to grow up is to accept vulnerability.
To be alive is to be vulnerable.

– MADELEINE L'ENGLE –

Discovering our Wildness,
we step towards our authentic self.
Yet can we find the courage to share this wild self with the world?
To reveal our undefended heart,
with all its doubt, uncertainty, longing and love?
To reclaim the power of Vulnerability
as the next step in our journey of transformation?

Learning Vulnerability: My Story

By September 2007, a year after the Marketing Forum, Wild Courage was just beginning to take hold. I had a handful of coaching clients, and was also beginning to build up experience in workshop facilitation. In 2007, an exciting opportunity came along that was both well paid and a topic I was passionate about: to facilitate a series of workshops to integrate sustainability into the strategy of all major brands in a large multi-national. It also meant working with a client (and friend) who I love and respect, in Rome, one of my favourite cities in the world. It looked good!

That two-day workshop dropped me into a steep tunnel of disappointment. I had envisaged a total overhaul of brand positioning and strategy; in reality the workshop involved a precise exploration of specific, tactical changes that the brand could make within the next few months. I could see the value of that, but it wasn't my passion. Meanwhile, I was also bumping up against the conservatism of the corporate world, as I saw it. This workshop had been running for some months, and followed a set format. I suggested we might introduce some creative techniques to help people come up with ideas in the breakout groups on the second day. It took a one-hour conversation with the core team, huddled in the middle of the room at the end of day one, to agree even this minor change. When it came to it, the other consultant working on the project avoided using the creative tools and reverted to the safe and familiar approach – simply 'discussing' ideas. I felt frustrated, powerless and undermined.

Behind the scenes, other vulnerabilities were playing themselves out. I had broken up with my boyfriend just two weeks before the workshop and was nursing a broken heart. I had hardly slept for weeks. Meanwhile, the client, was also facing challenges in his personal life and arrived at the workshop equally exhausted. The other team member, an external consultant who'd been developing the workshops for the last two years and was highly dependent on their income, no doubt had his own insecurities. Hiding behind 'professional' masks, none of us spoke to these vulnerabilities. They simply lurked under the surface.

By the end of the second day, I got on the airport bus feeling exhausted and flat. Sitting at the back, slightly nauseous as we wound through Rome's narrow streets, the client and I read the feedback forms. They were mixed – some had loved the workshop, others were neutral; some said the facilitation was inspiring and creative, others said I was too controlling. I felt slightly tearful. I am a perfectionist, and am used to getting rave reviews for the workshops I run! *Why didn't everyone like me? Had I failed? Was I good enough?* Not wanting to turn into these uncomfortable feelings, I pushed them away and headed to check-in.

As we walked to security with our wheelie bags in tow, a seemingly innocuous conversation pushed me over the edge. Amid the fluorescent lights and background hum of Fiumicino airport, the client, the external consultant and I began debriefing the workshop. 'I think it went well,' my client began. 'Yes, I agree,' the consultant replied, 'but I don't think the new brainstorming activities worked.' I felt like I'd been slapped. Those activities had been the only innovation I'd brought to the workshop; they were one of the few ways I felt I'd added value. Yet instead of sharing (or even registering) that I felt hurt by his words, my face flushed with rage and my body buzzed with adrenalin. Not only had this consultant gone against what we'd agreed as a team and boycotted the ideas I'd suggested, he now had the cheek to say that they hadn't worked! 'They might have worked if you'd tried them,' I told him as we headed towards the metal detectors at security. 'For me, if we agree to try something we should try it. To be honest, I feel kind of betrayed by you.' And then we walked through security, and left the conversation in midair as we headed towards our separate gates.

This is an uncomfortable story to tell. In many ways it's the perfect example of 'how not to do Vulnerability' and it's not flattering to my ego. I do realize that both my insecurities, and the suggestion of 'betrayal', flung out at airport security in the context of a relatively insignificant workshop, were mildly ridiculous! Yet this story is typical of so many. It is often relatively trivial things that finally push us over the edge into a vulnerability that has been building for days or weeks. And the way we respond is often just as the three of us responded: we ignore it.

The rest of that conversation never happened, at least not out in the open. The consultant complained to the client that I had been outspoken and disrespectful. Unable to connect by phone the client and I embarked on this difficult conversation by email – rarely a good idea. Misunderstandings and anger took hold amongst all three of us, and accusations, justifications and defences bounced across cyberspace, tangling our relationship into a tight, ugly ball.

Inside, I faced uncomfortable questions. Had I been I too aggressive? Why had I responded with anger, rather than sharing my vulnerability? Beyond these questions were other doubts. Could I continue with this project, having realized that a) it wasn't aligned with my passion and b) I did not respect all members of the team? On the other hand, could I afford to pull out of the rollout, risking tens of thousands of dollars of guaranteed income and potentially the relationship with a valued client and friend? Behind these questions lay deeper, unwanted vulnerabilities. Could the corporate world support my growing need to speak my truth, even when that truth was unwanted and challenging? Could I ever belong in an environment that valued safety and conformity, and frowned on risk, challenge and emotion? Was business the right place for me, or was I just attached to the financial reward of that work?

Frankly, these questions terrified me, and the implications threatened to throw my recently ordered world back into chaos. I faced a choice. I could turn away from these uncomfortable questions, reclaim my professional masks and head back onto solid ground. Or I could turn into my messy and frightening feelings, and follow them through to new ground. I chose the second way. Leaning into the darkness within, I opened to my vulnerability. I pulled out of the rollout of these workshops and opened the

110

trap door to the deeper feelings under the surface of my life. The journey was not easy, but it was alive, and its rough waves brought me into my heart and gave me new understanding, new strength and new language to express the sensitivity at my core.

After the Rome airport encounter, there were nine uncomfortable months where the relationship with my client–friend was on hold. Although I wanted to move straight to resolution, my client needed more time before he was ready to re-engage with me. It was a vulnerable place, in which I struggled with new, challenging questions: *Have I destroyed this friendship? Can I sit with the unresolved conflict even though my instinct is to try to 'make it better'? Can I trust the process to lead to resolution in its own time?* Eventually, many months later, I did meet with my client and we did turn into the courageous conversation. Reclaiming our vulnerabilities, we shared how we'd both been hurt by the encounter, what we'd learned, and how we needed to communicate in the future. And we reaped the rewards: deeper trust, compassion and appreciation for each other and the relationship.

The Nature of Vulnerability

> *There can be no vulnerability without risk.*
>
> – M SCOTT PECK

At our core, behind all our defences, is a soft, tender heart. Even the most tough, resilient, confident leader has this vulnerable underbelly. We all want to be loved. We all want to be good at what we do, to offer our selves to our work in a way that matters. We all want to feel fully alive in our hearts and bodies. Everyone has these longings – whether graduate trainee, cleaner, middle manager, PA or CEO.

Vulnerability comes from the Latin word *vulnus*, meaning 'wound'. To be vulnerable means to risk being wounded. It means living with an undefended heart, fully exposed to life with all its joys, adventures, losses and sorrows. To be vulnerable is to expose our tender underbelly to life and to others, to reveal our sensitivity, our love, our longings, our doubts, our fears and our uncertainties.

Although it's not always visible, Vulnerability is a natural and intrinsic part of everyday life. A number of things can bring it to the surface in our working world. Perhaps a changing business landscape threatens our job. Perhaps we feel out of our depth, struggling in new and unfamiliar territory. Perhaps, deep down, we question our suitability and capability to do our job. Perhaps we are going through a divorce, loss or trauma at home, and feel fragile even before we step into the office. Perhaps a team member, colleague or boss criticizes or overlooks us. Perhaps we simply feel tired. Any number of experiences and interactions can bring us into contact with our core vulnerability, leaving us exposed, naked and fragile.

What do we do with this Vulnerability? Often we just cover it up. So, walking around an office, we rarely see, hear or feel Vulnerability. We don't hear doubts – we hear answers. We don't see worries – we see solutions. We don't hear of sleepless nights – we observe the confident, collected façade. We don't feel vulnerable human beings – we see polished, professional, carbon-copy Super Leaders.

Defending against Vulnerability is a natural and instinctive response that also shows up widely across the natural world. Take, for example, porcupine, hedgehog and holly, who cover over their fragility with fierce, sharp spines and prickles. Or sea urchin, crab, armadillo and turtle, who protect a soft belly with a hard shell. Or creatures like snake, wasp, bee, jellyfish, poison oak and nettles, equipped with a stinging and sometimes deadly poison to protect themselves from predators. Or perhaps puffer fish, toads and certain corals, who blow themselves up to seem large and scary when they feel threatened. All these creatures have their own intricate way of protecting and disguising their vulnerability.

As humans, we have similar ways of protecting our tender hearts when we feel threatened or endangered, physically, emotionally, spiritually or intellectually. When something or someone touches a vulnerable place within us, we may react like a porcupine, bursting into a prickly bundle of sharp spines that keep the danger at a safe distance. In our case, those spines may be negativity, judgments, harsh words, irritation, obsessive busyness and restlessness. Other times we become more like a sea urchin, covering over our tenderness and wounding with a hard shell. For us, that shell might be boredom, denial, aloofness, coldness, depression and numbness. Or perhaps, like the wasp, we sting our 'predator', lashing out with anger, criticism, bitchiness, disdain and poisonous verbal attacks. Or maybe we respond like the puffer fish, blowing ourselves up with arrogance, self-importance, aloof authority and ego inflation. All these responses and behaviours are elaborate defence mechanisms that cover over and counterbalance hidden or unconscious feelings (or fears) of pain or wounding. They are all ways of keeping us from revealing or even experiencing our own vulnerability – masks we wear to protect our vulnerable core.

Other masks we wear are tied to the Camel leader within us. Highly aware of who we 'should' be and what we 'should' do, we strategically select personas that get us applause, recognition and love. We should be perfect. We should only speak out when we have something spectacularly intelligent to say. We should avoid the slightest risk of looking stupid. We should always appear to be in control. We should be rational and objective at all times. So we wear masks that make us appear to be these things.

Hiding behind these masks, we avoid exposing our true self. If we are rejected, it is the mask that is rejected. If we are not loved, it is the mask that is unlovable. That might be a little painful, yet it is far less painful than being rejected for who we really are. So our masks protect us from deeper wounding. From the point of view of the Protector within us, this makes sense. In fact, it's a pretty clever strategy. Yet it falls short in important ways. Refusing to claim our vulnerability, we lose the ability to connect and speak from a deeper, more intimate, unguarded place. We keep relationships neat yet distant; polite yet shallow; safe yet dull; smooth on the surface yet hollow inside.

Reclaiming Vulnerability

Honesty and transparency make you vulnerable.
Be honest and transparent anyway.

– MOTHER TERESA

In nature, protective mechanisms are survival strategies. For a turtle, a hard shell to hide behind can mean the difference between life and death. But what about in the human world? Do our defences against Vulnerability serve us in the same way?

For us, too, there are genuinely times when revealing our vulnerability is not safe and retreating behind armour is a healthy approach. Sometimes it's wisdom that stops us sharing our vulnerability, not fear – a sense that exposing our vulnerable core would be unhelpful or damaging. *Can I really trust this group of people to listen without judgment? Am I centred enough to speak my truth without attacking or blaming someone else? Will sharing these vulnerable feelings serve the group, the organization, society or life?* These are some of the questions that can help us know whether it's right to publicly expose our vulnerability – or whether we first need to process our feelings alone.

Defences are crucial when we are genuinely under attack. Yet the trouble is that our sense of danger is often highly exaggerated – and sometimes completely unfounded. What's more, old defence strategies remain long after they are necessary or useful, becoming habitual and unconscious. These outdated defences can hold us back in important ways.

Take, for example, a 30-year-old lawyer, Paula.[46] A high achiever constantly seeking to grow and develop, she decided to bring her annual appraisal to our coaching session. It was an excellent review that described her as a standout lawyer – and then went on to encourage her to be less reticent and reserved in meetings. 'What stops you speaking out in meetings?' I asked her. 'I'm afraid to look stupid,' she replied without blinking. 'Everyone else speaks perfect English, and I don't. I'm worried I'll make grammatical errors or that people will laugh at my accent. I'd rather be silent than be ridiculous.' Paula speaks near-perfect English, so the idea that people would laugh at her was, in itself, slightly ridiculous! 'So you don't want to risk being imperfect?' I challenged. She laughed and agreed. 'Do you remember when you first decided you needed to be perfect?' I continued. She closed her eyes and turned her attention inside. A few seconds later, her eyes popped open. 'It was when I was 15. I really fancied this boy at school. We had known each other for years and enjoyed hanging out together. One day I went to say hi to him on the school bus. He was with one of his new friends – part of the popular gang who saw me as shy and studious. After a few frosty words he just spat on me! I was mortified, but I didn't show it. Instead, I decided in that moment to become perfect, so that he would look at me and realize what he'd missed out on! I think I've been trying to be perfect ever since.'

Creating defences to avoid feeling rejected or inadequate might have been a necessary response for a 15-year-old. At the age of 30, though, Paula no longer needed to defend against these feelings. In fact, in order to grow into her fullness, she needed to be able to *tolerate* feelings of inadequacy; to confidently claim 'I am not perfect' and still feel loveable. This began with the smallest of actions: wearing a skirt for a day and exposing her 'imperfect' legs – something she had not done for 15 years. In this small yet defiant act, she made space for Vulnerability and, in doing so, found a new appreciation of her own power.

Paula's story highlights the subtle ways that outdated defences can hold us back. Other times, these old defences can be even more harmful – even poisonous. Often, they end up perpetuating the very thing we're trying to avoid. Holding people away from us, we become lonely – and hurt. Striking out with negativity or anger, we become unpopular – and hurt. Puffing ourselves up to seem confident and capable, we become isolated – and hurt. So our elaborate defences create the very thing they are trying to avoid – wounding. Over time, our whole emotional system shuts down, like a computer overloaded with too much unprocessed information. We shut out not only Vulnerability, but all feeling – and with it our passion, aliveness, sensitivity, love and joy. We become hard, rigid and unfeeling. Meanwhile, the wounds underneath our defences fester, leaving us hypersensitive to further wounding. So we may wildly overreact to the tiniest criticism, because it reminds us of criticism we experienced in the past. Or we may find ourselves frozen and resistant in times of change, because we haven't acknowledged the terror and grief of earlier experiences with change. Disowned, our feelings act out unconsciously, interrupting our relationships in strange and often ugly ways.

To bring this alive, let's look at the example of a young man born over a hundred years ago in Austria. In the two years before he was born, his parents lost three children, all of them under the age of two. So the birth of this young man was set against this backdrop of loss and grief, grief that may or may not have been acknowledged, processed and released. When he was 11 years old, his younger brother also died, aged just 5. After this, he went from a confident, outgoing boy who found school easy to a morose, detached, sullen boy who constantly battled his father and his teachers.[47] Then, at the age of 13, he lost his father, and four years later, his mother. By 17 he was an orphan, living in a homeless shelter with just one surviving sibling and a life that had already known much loss and hardship.

His response to all this loss and disappointment was to harden himself. As he writes in his autobiography: 'While the Goddess of Suffering took me in her arms, often threatening to crush me, my will to resistance grew, and in the end this will was victorious. I owe it to that period that I grew hard and am still capable of being hard.'[48] Later, further suffering would be piled on top of these childhood wounds – watching friends and comrades die while fighting in World War I, and later still, a year in prison as a political prisoner. These new wounds would solidify into rage, covering over his pain and vulnerability with an empowering sense of judgment, outrage and hatred.

The story, as you may have guessed, is the story of Adolf Hitler. We all know how it unfolded and the horrific acts that were later sanctioned under his leadership. I don't share his childhood to excuse his actions or justify them. I share Hitler's story, rather, as an extreme example of the suffering we can cause when we don't attend to our own pain, and when we allow adversity and difficulty to close and harden our hearts. In *Mein Kampf*, Hitler writes: 'In the case of such a person, the hard struggle through which he passes often destroys his normal human sympathy. His own fight kills his sensibility for the misery of those who have been left behind.'[49] Although he is referring to other people (those who struggle to improve their social status), Hitler's words could as easily describe himself and his own response to the struggle and misery of his early life. His story is a stark reminder of the dangers of excluding Vulnerability from our work and leadership.

How, then, do we reclaim our vulnerability? Can we find the courage to strip away the masks and defences that hide the tenderness of our soul from the world? Can we dare to accept our vulnerability and risk the nakedness it demands?

One of my coaching clients faced exactly this challenge. Recruited as CEO of a rather traditional organization, he found himself confronting a very difficult question: *Is this organization still valuable or is it time to dissolve it?* Owning this question cast him into a vulnerable role – a role in which he might, potentially, have to make unpopular decisions and risk being disliked, judged and rejected by hundreds of employees. So he kept the question to himself, hidden underneath a sunny exterior.

As he befriended his new team, he was aware of the duplicity of his intentions. In public, he wore the mask of Cheerleader – positive, supportive, likeable. Behind the scenes, aware of the possibility that he might have to cut jobs and maybe even dissolve the whole organization, he was an Executioner – detached, critical and ruthless. Neither of these masks expressed his true, more vulnerable experience: a new leader who wanted to do the right thing for the organization and a human being who wanted to be loved. As he became aware of this vulnerability, he was able to move beyond it. That meant leaving behind the masks of Cheerleader and Executioner and speaking openly with his core leadership team about his plans, doubts and concerns. Making space for this honesty risked a painful and difficult conversation. Yet it also built trust, which strengthened team relationships far more effectively than the false optimism of his Cheerleader mask.

As this story shows, stepping out from behind our masks is as simple (and as terrifying) as speaking our truth. That means daring to reveal our true beliefs, feelings and values – even when that truth is unpopular, unwanted or uncomfortable. Speaking our truth, we stand, exposed, naked and defenceless. We risk rejection – not of our masks, but of our true self. That, of course, is deeply vulnerable – and therefore deeply courageous.

However much we try to avoid Vulnerability, the working world draws us towards it, asking us to step into courageous and vulnerable conversations. These conversations can happen in both momentous and mundane encounters. Perhaps at a meeting with the board, we have to speak out and risk being judged. Or in a performance review with a boss or team member, we have to give difficult feedback and risk being disliked. Or in a presentation to shareholders or clients, we have to admit that we don't have all the answers and risk being dismissed. Or any other conversation where we expose our true self. If you're struggling to identify a conversation, you might ask yourself: *What am I pretending not to notice?* The answer to that question will almost always point you firmly in the direction of a vulnerable conversation waiting to happen.

What usually marks a courageous conversation is that we'd rather not have it – yet we know we need to. Not surprising, then, that in the seconds before we speak we may feel our heart beating heavily in our chest; we may become breathless or experience other symptoms of anxiety. Still, despite the fear, we feel compelled to speak out. Sometimes, this is an intuitive feeling, a sense that 'something needs to be said', even if we're not quite sure why. Other times it's the grumblings of our body that compel us to speak. Other times it's simply the intensity of our feelings. Other times it's a sleepless night and feeling of restlessness that propels us into a more vulnerable and truthful exchange. All these symptoms point us towards the frightening yet exhilarating experience of dropping our masks and revealing our true self.

The Vulnerability of the Unknown

The true role of a leader of a creative system
is not to foresee and take control of its journey, but to contain
the anxiety of its members as they
operate at the edge of chaos where they are creating and
discovering a new future that none could possibly foresee.

– RALPH STACEY

One mask many of us hide behind is the Powerful Leader. Usually this means maintaining authority by directing, controlling, keeping it together and always having the answers. This may tick all the boxes of a 'good' leader, and it may seem to generate authority. Yet, when we find ourselves leading in changing or uncertain times, this mask becomes problematic. Deep down, everyone knows we don't have the answers. If we refuse to drop the false mask of Powerful Leader and keep pretending we know everything, ultimately we will look stupid. Although it may feel counterintuitive and risky, claiming our vulnerability is actually the only way to establish authority in a changing world. To be truly credible, we must be able to say:

'This is what I do know . . . and this is what I don't.'

Richard Hytner shared a story of this kind of vulnerable leadership, in our conversation about Stillness. In a presentation to 70 or 80 of Saatchi & Saatchi's leadership team in 2009, Richard told me, the managing director publicly shared his fear and uncertainty. His presentation went something like this: 'The financial world is in crisis. The advertising world is in crisis. I don't know about you, but I'm terrified. Fifty million people worldwide have lost their jobs. That's pretty scary – and if you're not scared, you should be. And the truth is, we don't know what to do. I'm f***ing CEO, and I don't know what to do. Quite probably, you have a better idea than I do. So let's just get on with it, and figure it out together.' Having shared his radical vulnerability, the MD then went on to add a few known parameters, to give some definition to the uncertainty. 'Here are a few signposts. What we do know is this. We are Saatchi & Saatchi. This is how we do things round here . . .' and he shared a few key points about the company and its way of doing things. 'So as long as what you do in some way supports that idea, you can do what you like. And you can fail – just fail cheaply!'[50]

After he told me this story, Richard continued: 'Afterwards, there was an enormous sense of relief. And later, when we shared the DVD with the team in India, it got a standing ovation. It was almost like giving everyone permission to fess up to not knowing! And there was a huge relief, because if the CEO fesses up to us, then we can fess up to our clients. We can all stop pretending that we know what's happening in the market or how to reinvent ourselves for a changing world. And so – here's the really important part – we can have a crack at it. We can figure it out, and find new ways, together.' As this story shows, dropping the mask of Powerful Leader, acknowledging we don't have all the answers, does not mean we publicly collapse in despair and hopelessness. Instead, we claim our vulnerability with power – and in so doing, we hold on to, and even strengthen, our authority and credibility as a leader.

When we drop our habitual masks and open to our vulnerability, we inevitably encounter new and less developed parts of our inner world. As the ground moves around us, old techniques, habits and strategies are now revealed as too small, no longer relevant. They no longer get results; they no longer help us navigate this new and shifting terrain. This can be deeply uncomfortable. If the right side of the body is strong and powerful, then writing, playing sport or leaning on the left side may feel awkward and frustrating. The same is true with our inner world. There, too, developing new skills and resources may leave us feeling small, inadequate, clumsy and frustrated.

One client I work with is a brilliant strategic thinker, full of integrity, kind and polite. These gifts helped him build his own business and turn it into a dynamic and respected agency. For many years, being brilliant with strategy and great with clients was enough. Yet after 15 years of this, he started to bump up against frustration and exhaustion. Looking behind these feelings, he discovered an underlying, unspoken conflict with one of his business partners. His expertise in strategy and client relationships didn't equip him for this kind of conversation. So he faced a choice: to turn away and head back towards familiar terrain where he was confident and expert – or to become a beginner and to learn the new language of Vulnerability and feeling. Choosing Vulnerability, he set up a series of conversations with his business partner to address the issues in the relationship. Going a step further, he named his lack of experience and discomfort with addressing these kinds of conflicts and asked his partner to be patient as he learned this new, more emotional language.

This story highlights our core challenge in the face of Vulnerability. Do we keep playing to our strengths, leaning on the parts of us that have historically helped us to become successful? Or do we move towards less developed parts of our selves, even when that leaves us feeling exposed? Can we find the courage to reclaim our vulnerability, with all its terror, beauty and life?

The Gifts of Vulnerability

You have been telling the people that this
is the Eleventh Hour.
Now you must go back and tell the people
that this is The Hour.
And there are things to be considered:
Where are you living?
What are you doing?
What are your relationships?
Are you in right relation?

– HOPI ELDERS

Why would we open to Vulnerability and willingly risk being wounded? Why abandon our defences? Why drop our masks and stand naked, defence-less and exposed? Surely that is a crazy idea? Well, yes, from the point of view of the Protector, who likes to keep life safe and neatly ordered between straight lines. Yes for the Powerful Leader who needs to appear resilient, tough and certain. But not for the soul. Not for the soulful leader.

The soul is not interested in being tough or hard. It wants to come alive – to experience life's full range of experiences and emotions. It wants to drop all masks and come into contact directly with life, whatever the conse-quences. Sometimes that brings us to the exalted, the beautiful, the magnificent, the touching – other times it brings us to darker, more chal-lenging places. To the soul, these experiences are equally valuable. The soul is not interested in defending against change or numbing feeling so as to move quickly back into productive activity. It doesn't need to tidy up the grief of a wounded heart, cover over inadequacy or head back onto solid ground. It wants to feel the full impact of changes and crises. It wants to turn towards powerlessness, rejection, betrayal, loss and abandonment and use these feelings as a gateway into an inner journey. Through that inner journey, with its winding streets of grief, despair, rage and inadequacy, we are broken open into life. For the soul, *this* is success.

We find many gifts on this journey into Vulnerability. The first is a renewed sense of energy and power. Holding onto masks and defences takes a huge amount of energy. When we drop our defences and lean into our vulnerability, we free up this energy – to live, to love, to find new, creative and imaginative ways of being in the world, to focus on the task at hand. Over time, we also start to develop a greater faith in our self and in life. Often we are surprised by our ability to withstand so much wounding: to keep moving into the murkiness of a changing world; to be broken open by change and not numb out; to willingly stay present with life, wherever it takes us, over and over, time after time.

As we open to our wounds and trust ourselves to follow this dangerous and challenging journey, we start to feel a new sense of safety. Having lived through difficult feelings and experiences, we develop faith in ourselves. We realize: *Whatever happens, I will be okay. There may be grief, loss, sorrow, despair, terror, rage – yet I can navigate these difficult places.* As superficial identities and images of ourselves fall away or are broken down, we come face to face with a naturally resilient quality within us – our essence. Unexpectedly, living with Vulnerability makes us far more resilient than the superficial mask of Powerful Leader.

Vulnerability also brings trust and integrity to our relationships. We may fear that speaking our truth will destroy our relationships by hurting other people, undermining our authority or simply stopping us getting our to-do list done. But in reality, when offered sensitively and without blame, sharing our vulnerability strengthens our relationships, our reputation and even our ability to get the job done. When we speak our truth, and when that truth is received with an open heart, we learn to trust our colleagues and relationships more deeply. We stop trying to be perfect and we relax, realizing that even with all our flaws we are not beyond love. So we feel seen, appreciated, accepted and valued for who we are – and we shower our love, gratitude and gifts on the relationship. What's more, as we reclaim our vulnerability, we make space for others to do the same. As we drop our masks, we invite others to drop theirs. And so we start to co-create a deeper, more intimate, less guarded work environment in which creative ideas can take hold and projects can run smoothly and efficiently.

Feeling and healing our wounds also develops compassion. Compassion comes from the Latin *compati*, which means 'to suffer with' (*com-*, with, and *-pati*, to suffer). Knowing what it is to feel pain, grief, loss, despair and loneliness, we are able to 'suffer with' and empathize with others in these places. If we are able to feel our own grief, we can allow and support others' grief. If we acknowledge our own rage, we can meet others' anger without fear. If we know despair, we can support others in despair without judgment. As leaders, that means we can support a greater emotional range in ourselves and our team. Integrating our vulnerability, we become generous, compassionate leaders.

Opening to difficult and painful feelings also has benefits on a larger scale. 'How do we live with the fact that we are destroying our world?' eco-philosopher Joanna Macy asks. Her answer is – we deny it. We refuse to acknowledge it, and we bury our grief, rage and despair. 'We create diversions for ourselves as individuals and as nations, in the fights we pick, the aims we pursue, and the stuff we buy . . . (and so) the energy expended in pushing down despair is diverted from more crucial uses, depleting the resilience and imagination needed for fresh visions and strategies.'[51] Macy's words hint at another gift of Vulnerability – the ability to compassionately acknowledge our (often destructive) impact on the planet and to seek out new, sustainable ways of living and working. What if we didn't ship our overflowing waste to the developing world, but were confronted with the consequences of our throwaway culture? What if we saw the children making our cheap clothes, or spoke to the relatives of the 760,000 people who die in China every year from air and water pollution?[52] What if we spoke with someone who could, for the first time in generations, feed and educate her child with the income from her job in that same factory? If we got this personal, would we still be able to numb out from the confusion and complexity of our changing world? Or would we turn into the vulnerability – the longing, grief, guilt, pain, despair, rage and confusion – and there find new approaches, insights and solutions to the economic, environmental and social challenges of our time?

Ray Anderson's story shows what's possible when we enter into this vulnerable relationship with the earth. Anderson is CEO of Interface, the largest carpet manufacturer in the world. His journey into Vulnerability began when he read Paul Hawken's *The Ecology of Commerce*, and began to see the earth as a delicate ecosystem rather than a series of resources to be used by humans. Through this new lens, Anderson realized: 'In another world, perhaps not far from now, what I do will become illegal.' If the earth had rights, he and his company were violating them.

Claiming this vulnerable insight, Anderson made a courageous confession. Addressing civic and business leaders at North Carolina State University in 1995, he publicly declared: 'I stand convicted by me myself alone as a plunderer of the earth. But not by our civilization's definition. By our civilization's definition I am a captain of industry, in the eyes of many a kind of modern-day hero. . . . But really . . . really? The first industrial revolution is flawed. It is not working. It is unsustainable. It is the mistake. And we must move on to another and better industrial revolution and get it right this time.'[53]

The value of Anderson's vulnerability can be measured in the changes and progress made at Interface. Since 1995, when Anderson made that speech, Interface has reduced its ecological footprint by one-third. Practically, that means using and reusing the raw materials they extract from the earth. It means using renewable energy. It means a simple yet powerful innovation that ensures carpet tiles are easily swappable, so that if one section gets damaged only a small portion needs to be replaced. And it means exploring other, even more fundamental changes in the structure of the business – for example, a business model in which people lease carpets rather than buy them, so that old carpets can be reused and recycled rather than simply thrown into a land-fill site. Change rarely happens overnight, and as Anderson says, Mount Sustainability is higher than Mount Everest. Interface still has some way to go before it reaches its publicly stated intent to be 'an organization of people committed to a purpose of doing no harm', fully sustainable, with zero eco-logical footprint, by 2020. Yet the changes Anderson and his team have ini-tiated are impressive first steps up that mountain.[54]

When Zen monk Thich Nhat Hanh was asked, 'What do we most need to do to save our world?' he answered: 'What we most need to do is to hear within us the sounds of the Earth crying.'[55] When we drop into our vulner-ability, we can do just this. Connected to our hearts, we find compassion and connection with *all* species, *all* living beings. We no longer see the world as a series of resources, at our disposal. Nor do we see it as something *out there*, to be used, trampled on or controlled. Instead, we fall in love with this web of vibrant, interconnected, interdependent organisms, of which we are just one tiny part. And so, reclaiming our vulnerability not only gifts us with courage, faith and resilience. It not only gifts our relationships with intimacy, trust and respect. It is also our gift back to life, to this beautiful green-blue earth we call home. Broken open into Vulnerability, we soften into our hearts and open the way to deep and lasting change.

Vulnerable Leadership

Scott Eberle, Hospice Physician

A hospice physician based in Petaluma, California, Scott also runs programs with the School of Lost Borders in the Practice of Living and Dying – including the Great Ballcourt Vision Quest that I attended in 2009. He is a man with an enormous heart. Vulnerability is perhaps not a quality we readily associate with medical professionals. To survive the physical and emotional demands of the job, most physicians learn to be tough and resilient. In the average working day, there is no time for doubt, uncertainty or an emotional response to the crises they face. The doctor's role is to stay calm in times of crisis and navigate difficult and emotional situations with a detached kind of authority.

More often than not, to stay safely on this pedestal of 'authority', physicians learn to override their vulnerability. As Scott says: 'At med school, we were taught that authority came from facts, information and knowledge. Even if we didn't really know the facts, we were taught to speak with authority, often hiding behind a kind of false bravado. As doctors, our role was to have the answers. It was as simple as that. We were expected to shut down our hearts and stay objective and rational at all times.'

From the start of his medical career, Scott's experiences threw him into a different kind of relationship with power and Vulnerability. He happened to go through med school in San Francisco during the HIV epidemic of 1982–1986. Later, he did his residency in Santa Rosa, where HIV was also prolific. Back then, there were very few medical facts to offer people living with AIDS, and the prognosis was often a year or two at best. So from the start, the source of authority Scott had been taught at medical school (medical facts) was turned upside down. He could master the facts that were available, but beyond that, the most valuable thing he could offer was an open heart, a willingness to listen to his patients' stories and help them die with respect and dignity.

Twenty-five years later, these lessons in Vulnerability still run through Scott's ethos and practice. As a hospice physician there are of course often times when Scott needs to be directive – mostly when offering prognosis and agreeing a treatment plan. Yet direction is only part of the story. 'Contrary to what we were taught in med school, I don't believe that true authority comes from having all the answers. Instead it comes from being able to hold the chaos of very difficult situations and stay present in the uncertainty.' As a physician that means being equally comfortable with the known and the unknown so that we can share both. 'We need to master all the facts, and to own our wisdom and power. Yet we also need to be able to say when we don't have the answers. Ultimately, this generates more authority than fragile, false bravado where we pretend to have all the answers.'

Scott's work as a hospice physician also demands another kind of Vulnerability – the Vulnerability of being fully present with another human being in intense and challenging situations. To do that, Scott needs to be able to feel as well as to think, to connect emotionally with his patients as well as holding a more detached perspective. As he says: 'When I'm at the bedside of someone who's dying, there is an expectation that I can hold, feel, direct and shape what may be a very chaotic story. And to do that well, I have to risk being touched, to feel the joy and suffering of another person's story.'

What are the implications of integrating Vulnerability into our leadership and work? In Scott's experience, owning Vulnerability has meant a complete reorganization of his professional life. To listen and stay present with his patients, in both their joy and pain, Scott needs to be able to put his own story and feelings aside temporarily. And to stay connected with his Vulnerability, he needs to consciously make time and space to come back to those feelings. Knowing this, Scott has designed his professional life so that there is space for Stillness – for quiet reflective time where he can open his heart to his own feelings.

For him, that means sitting in meditation twice a day, and two or three times a year going away on week-long retreats. It has also meant making sacrifices. Rather than maximizing income, Scott has created a working week that is more open, spacious and flexible than the average physician's. This is a conscious choice, allowing him time and space to process his own emotions so that he can stay centred and present in the chaotic and vulnerable situations his job presents.

Being willing to feel the intense vulnerability of being with people who are dying also brings many gifts to his work with the living. In his work as a wilderness rites of passage guide, Scott holds other chaotic stories – the stories of change and transition from one life stage to another. Opened and softened by his work with the dying, Scott is able to hold these people safely, tenderly and fiercely through change into a new cycle of life. In touch with the innate Vulnerability of being human, Scott is able to make space for others to hold and reclaim the vulnerability of their own human expereince.

Living (or dying) with Vulnerability is not always easy. As Scott says: 'Developing Vulnerability means exploring this question of how to be human. And month to month, year to year, I'm still learning.'

Source: My interview with Scott Eberle

PRACTICE # 5

Council*

The practice of Council, creating circles for sharing and listening, is a great way of consciously making space to speak from the heart and share the vulnerability of our full truth. Council is based on the traditional practice of bringing issues, challenges and conflicts to a council of the elders. Sitting in a circle where every member of the community has a chance to speak, the wise men and women of the tribe offer a space in which every voice can be heard.

Council offers a safe way of bringing different, and sometimes conflicting, voices into the conversation in a safe and productive way. Slowing the conversation down, it allows us to see many angles and perspectives on a situation, decision or relationship and to bring to the surface the richness of these different opinions. In Council, there is no judgement, nor is there any expectation to 'resolve' the issues that are raised. The intention of Council is simply to create a space for each voice to be witnessed. Holding each perspective with respect and appreciation makes it safe to share more Vulnerable feelings and opinions with the group. And when each person feels deeply heard, shifts in perspective and relationship happen naturally.

Council can be used in a number of ways in the working world. It could be offered as a way to explore team dynamics and strengthen relationships within a team; as an opportunity to share reactions and feelings during organization change or other business challenges; for conflict resolution; or simply as a creative technique for strategic visioning and idea generation. For example, in a brand-positioning project with a New York-based cable TV channel, Council created space for a team of highly successful, fast-paced New Yorkers to slow down the conversation and to really listen to each perspective in the room. It encouraged the team to speak from their hearts, sharing what really mattered to them rather than just intellectual views and opinions. Common themes and dreams emerged, and within them, the new brand positioning became clear.

An extremely simple tool, Council is nonetheless extremely effective – even beyond the bounds of the formal practice. When we adhere to Council's four basic principles in our everyday conversations with peers, bosses, subordinates and teams, we integrate Vulnerability and its gifts into the culture of our team and organization. It becomes kind of a background hum, a subtle thread in the fabric of our organizational culture.

When you first start creating space for Council, you may want to work with an experienced facilitator to help you navigate any difficult conversations and conflicts that emerge. However, if you do want to experiment with Council by yourself, here are some guidelines.

1. Create a circle with your team (preferably with no tables in the middle) and clarify your **intention** or question for the Council to explore. Set up the Council by sharing the four guidelines and making agreements on Confidentiality.

2. Choose an object as your **'talking piece'**. During Council, only the person holding the talking piece can talk. Everyone else listens. After speaking, place the talking piece back in the centre of the circle, where someone else can claim it. If you're short of time, you may prefer to simply pass the talking piece clockwise around the circle. People may choose to 'pass' if they're not ready to speak, and you may find it useful to pass the stick twice around the circle, to ensure everyone has shared what they need and want to share.

3. Introduce **the four basic principles of Council**:
   * **Show up** – really show up, without your masks and with nothing defending the tenderness and strength of your soul.
   * **Speak from the heart**, sharing your whole truth, while keeping

to the heart of the matter and being as concise as possible.

 ⁕ **Listen from the heart**, genuinely listening to what is said, even if you need to drop your habitual perspectives and beliefs to hear it.

 ⁕ **Be spontaneous**, letting things unfold in their own way. Stay open to being surprised by where you end up.

4. Open the circle by stating the group's intention. Then place the talking piece in the centre. **Encourage each person to take the talking piece and share** their perspective. Listen openly and with full attentiveness to each one. Ideally, each sharing will build on the previous sharings.

5. When everyone has shared and you feel that the intention has been met, **close the Council** and the conversation. All conversations should be held as sacred and confidential – not picked up again outside of the circle or discussed privately among fragments of the group.

* Thanks to the School of Lost Borders, Gigi Coyle, Marlow Hotchkiss and Kerry Brady for introducing me to this powerful and beautiful tool.

CHAPTER 6

Surrender

Entering the Flow of Soul

*We must be willing to let go
of the life we have planned,
so as to have the life that is waiting for us.*

– E M FORSTER –

So we come to the final step
in the journey of transformation:
Surrender.
Stepping into the currents of change,
we merge our dreams and visions
with the larger story of life.
What new power might we discover
in this act of Surrender?

Opening to Surrender: My Story

Every stage of my journey into change involved Surrender. There was surrendering to Dying, leaving behind the safety of Unilever to enter into a new, creative flow. There was surrendering to the Stillness of the Threshold, to the mystery of Intuition, to Wildness and its longings. And, of course, there was the surrender into Vulnerability and the dark inner journey it led me on. Without Surrender, none of these moves would have been possible.

By 2009, five years after my first step into this journey of change, I had hit a wall. My life had changed beyond recognition; so too had my sense of identity. The fast-paced high achiever had softened into a deep, compassionate, intuitive (and still sometimes fierce) woman. Yet somehow I felt stuck in this inner journey, unable to fully emerge into life and offer my full powers back to the world. The evidence for this was subtle. I was earning enough money, and I had good projects and clients; yet I simply felt, quietly and intuitively, that there was more I could give. I just didn't know how to step into it.

In the summer of 2009 I found myself in Big Pine, California, on my first Vision Quest. Whilst other participants were there to find their way through divorce, retirement or even cancer, I was there to cross a more subtle threshold: to mark the end of a long, introspective period of 'Dying', and a readiness to step back out into new life. To do that, I was willing to face the terrifying proposition of a four day and four night 'solo': sleeping alone in the wilderness of the Inyo Mountains, with no food, no company and no shelter. What would I do in those four days? How would I feel without food? Was it safe? Did I need to worry about mountain lions, scorpions and snakes? I didn't know. I simply knew it was time to leave behind the fading structures and beliefs of my current reality (this time as spiritual seeker, student, apprentice) and to step courageously across the threshold into a new life. I knew that I needed something fierce and precise to mark my willingness to step into the next movement of my life. And I'd heard that a Vision Quest might help.

Those days were empty, boring, slow, intense, emotional and alive. I left Big Pine opened – still unsure what my next step might be, yet willing to surrender into it. Three months later, that commitment to Surrender was tested. I was on my way back from facilitating a two-day workshop in India. It had been a chaotic and intense experience, with 18 leaders, jet lag and inevitable bouts of Indian food poisoning. Added to that, we'd had the worry of heightened terror alerts. By the end of our third day, my co-facilitator and I were immensely relieved to flop safely onto our British Airways flatbeds and head home to London.

It was 3am when we finally took off from Mumbai, and I was already falling towards sleep. In the upper deck, the cabin was hushed, filled with other business passengers who looked as exhausted as I felt. A seasoned traveller, I'm generally relaxed about flying, so even before the seatbelt signs had been switched off, I had converted my seat into an extremely welcome bed. Snuggled under a blanket with my sleeper suit, eye mask and earplugs, I only half-registered the captain's announcement: 'Senior cabin crew to the flight deck immediately'. It was only when I heard the next announcement that I bothered to sit up: 'Cabin crew, take your positions.' As I peered out from behind my dividing screen, I saw the cabin crew standing nervously in the aisle, and I knew that things were not right.

Over the next minutes, it emerged that the plane's wheels had been damaged during takeoff. The extent of the damage was not clear, and we did not know whether we would be able to land safely or not. Either way, we had to head back to Mumbai and make an emergency landing. First, though, we had to dump our excess fuel into the ocean (poor ocean) to be light enough to land. According to the captain, that would take about an hour.

For that next hour, I stared death in the face. As the cabin crew briefed us on the brace position and emergency protocol, the fear in their voices was palpable. Suspended in a metal box in the sky, there was a single, unspoken thought: *Is this the last hour of my life?* With my co-facilitator seated downstairs, I was in the upper deck with just eight other business travellers.

There was no shouting, no crying, no hugs, no drama of any kind. One by one, people quietly got ready for the emergency landing, getting their passports and credit cards out of overhead lockers, changing out of sleeping suits and asking the cabin crew questions on evacuation procedure. The man in front of me turned around and pulled a face, as if to say: *This is all a bit weird, isn't it?* People turned on phones and Blackberrys and began sending messages to loved ones back home.

Throughout that hour of waiting, my body buzzed with adrenalin. At first, I wondered if I should text anyone. But I'd already tied up loose ends in my relationships in preparing for my Vision Quest just a few months before, so on reflection, that didn't seem necessary. I turned to other activities – changing back into jeans, filling my pockets with passport, phone and credit card, clearing the space around my seat and calculating and recalculating my quickest route to the emergency exit. Staying busy, maybe I could avoid facing the true impact of this frightening and vulnerable situation.

At some point there was nothing more to do but wait. I closed my eyes and allowed my mind to flick through a filing cabinet of memories. Even as I reviewed my life, the adrenalin in my body and the longing in my heart told me I wasn't ready to die. As the captain announced that we would be touching down in five minutes, fear took on a tighter grip. My head felt cloudy and my heart was pounding in my chest. *So this is what fear feels like,* I thought. And then I found myself thinking: *If I'm going to die, I want to be conscious.* And just like that, the fog cleared in my head, and I felt a new sense of calm and space.

As we descended, I watched the light on the wing flashing through dense clouds of white smoke. I adopted the brace position, and I surrendered. It wasn't a passive kind of surrender – a giving up, a willingness to die. Within it, there was still an incredible force for life, a readiness to run towards the emergency exit and sprint fast and furious away from a burning plane and into my future. But within that fierce passion for life, there was also a quiet knowing that the power to live was only partly mine. I could run, yes. I could hold on to a determination to live and a belief that it was possible. But I couldn't stop the plane bursting into flames as it touched down, if that was what was going to happen. I could manoeuvre events to some extent, but I also had to accept that there were forces greater and more powerful than my ego – and I had no choice but to give myself to them.

The plane landed bumpily with fire engines at the ready, but it landed safely. I stepped off that plane knowing, in every cell of my body, what it felt like to want something so deeply, and still allow space for Surrender; to give my dreams over to something bigger than me, to trust in a destiny that I was only co-authoring with life. This initiation into Surrender stayed with me and informed my life and work long after we safely touched down in London.

The Nature of Surrender

> *There is a river flowing now very fast.*
> *It is so great and swift,*
> *that there are those who will be afraid.*
> *They will try to hold on to the shore.*
> *They will feel they are being torn apart*
> *and will suffer greatly.*
> *Know the river has its destination.*

– HOPI ELDERS

Thirteen billion years ago, according to the most recent guess, the universe came forth as a fiercely hot cluster of elementary particles, denser than lead. For three hundred thousand years, it expanded until it cooled enough to form atoms. As those atoms cooled and expanded, they formed over a hundred billion huge clouds that we call 'galaxies'. Over time, these galaxies became more complex, birthing stars. These burning stars transformed the elements at their core, turning the hydrogen into helium into carbon.

Eventually the stars and their elements exploded, forming planets. Three and half billion years ago, life formed in at least one of these planetary systems – Earth. And as the universe continued to evolve and emerge, ever more complex life forms showed up on planet Earth, eventually becoming multicellular beings, with cells and nuclei.[56] Two hundred thousand years ago, humans became part of this story.

This story reminds us that we live in an inherently creative universe – and that, as evolutionary cosmologist Brian Swimme points out, 'most of the creativity of the universe took place without hands and without brains'.[57] Life has been evolving for billions of years, and we are only a tiny part in its journey. Somehow, though, when it comes to the challenges of our own lives and our own societies, we forget this. We think that we are in charge, that we have to figure out the answers alone. We forget that the challenges and dilemmas we face are part of a much larger story, a much deeper movement – a process of evolution that extends back further than we can imagine. We are just one intricate and important piece in this vast, wise and naturally creative universe. We are not running the show.

When we surrender, we give ourselves to this natural movement of life. We step into life's flow, and we merge our dreams and actions with a deeper sense of life's journey. We let go of our own agenda, and lean into the primal creativity of the universe. We might call this primal creativity by any number of names, depending on our belief system: God, Allah, creativity, creative emergence, destiny, Universal Love, or simply Life. Indeed, many religions speak of Surrender. *Islam* literally translates as 'resignation, surrendering', and salaaming, bowing the head and body towards the earth, is a gesture of this surrender to God. The Lord's Prayer declares: 'Thy will be done.' In the Hopi poem shared at the beginning of this book, the elders of this indigenous tribe remind us: 'Know the river has its destination . . . let go of the shore, push into the middle of the river.' Whatever language we frame it in, surrendering means dropping into life's natural movement and flow, offering our ego and will to that greater movement.

Surrendering drops us back into a bigger picture and allows us to take our place in a story that spans species, continents and generations. When we surrender, the question we ask ourselves is no longer *What do I want to happen?* or *What do I want to create?* Instead, it becomes *What wants to happen here – and how can I participate in that movement?* Engaging with this question, we offer our creative abilities in service to the bigger story, addressing not only our own needs but also the needs of life.

As we surrender, we open to life unconditionally, allowing ourselves to be taken to experiences that we might 'prefer' to avoid. Instead of trying to direct, control or eradicate an unwanted experience or an uncomfortable feeling, we ask: *What is right about this – no matter how wrong it seems to my ego? What does my soul want me to learn here?* Placing our trust in the wisdom of life, we open to discover the gift within these unwanted experiences.

Rumi speaks of the gift of surrendering into our feelings, even those that are 'unwanted guests', in his poem 'The Guest House'.

> This being human is a guest house.
> Every morning a new arrival.
>
> A joy, a depression, a meanness,
> some momentary awareness comes
> as an unexpected visitor.
>
> Welcome and entertain them all!
> Even if they're a crowd of sorrows,
> who violently sweep your house
> empty of its furniture,
> still, treat each guest honourably.
> He may be clearing you out
> for some new delight.
>
> The dark thought, the shame, the malice,
> meet them at the door laughing,
> and invite them in.

> Be grateful for whoever comes,
> because each has been sent
> as a guide from beyond.[58]

As Rumi's words suggest, even the most uncomfortable, unwanted feeling can bring unexpected gifts, teaching and wisdom. If we listen to it, rage can show us where our boundaries are being violated. Grief can help us connect to a deep, unmet longing. Despair can lead us to compassion and new hope. Surrendering means opening our heart to all these guests until we discover the gift they bring.

As we stop struggling against what is, and accept it as the gateway into something new, we follow our feelings along a winding path into our emerging future. Making friends with each situation as just another colour of life, we catch a glimpse of a bigger picture, of the positive possibilities of even the most challenging, frightening and unwanted experiences. So we grow and evolve. New paths open up. New possibilities present themselves. New solutions to the challenges of our time become available. We enter into a larger relationship with life.

Reclaiming Surrender

> *Crazed, lying in a zero circle, mute,*
> *We shall be saying finally,*
> *With tremendous eloquence, Lead us.*

> – RUMI

Surrender is not a hugely popular concept in the working world, where personal power and control are seen as the path to promotion, recognition and success. Terrified to even contemplate powerlessness, we turn away from Surrender and head stubbornly towards control, often at the expense of Life. We forge our way into new markets, even when those markets are dying or destructive to the bigger story. We push through our five-year plan, even when the world around us shows that it's flawed, outdated or harmful. We struggle with each other and our competitors, even when collaboration across organizations, political parties and nations is clearly called for. We push our own agenda, even when the team, organization, society and planet are screaming for cooperation.

Recent New Age teachings have exacerbated our tendency to see ourselves as all-powerful beings. Best-selling books on the Law of Attraction, hypnotherapy and neuro-linguistic programming promise us the power to manifest our dreams. And it is, of course, true. The creative power of the human being is immense, and we can indeed manifest our visions and dreams into reality with the power of intent and imagination. Yet there is another paradoxical truth: that we are powerless to forces beyond our control. There are forces at work in the universe that we do not direct, forces we cannot understand, see or measure. We are shaped and moved by these forces just as much as (perhaps even more than) we are shaped or moved by our own individual will. So the challenge is to hold the tension between our power and our powerlessness: to honour both, to accept both, to claim both.

Reclaiming Surrender means finding a middle ground between control and passivity. We don't collapse into a state of helplessness, powerlessness or blame, withdrawing from life and abdicating responsibility for our actions and choices. Nor do we inflate our ego with an exaggerated sense of our own power, and use that power to manifest wholly selfish goals and dreams. After all, as Brian Swimme says, the universe has been evolving for 13 billion years; it's unlikely its ultimate goal is consumerism![59]

When we surrender, we participate actively in the deeper movements of life without directing them. We connect with life's shifting currents and listen intuitively for what wants to emerge. Then, and only then, do we draw on the power of our will and direct our energies towards manifesting our goals and intentions. Surrendering into the creative flow, we become a channel through which life can emerge, change and evolve. In that new relationship with power and creativity, we find purpose, aliveness, ease and flow.

Surrendering drops us into the current of life's primal creativity. Any number of artists have spoken and written of this, and the same experience is available to us, whatever work we're engaged with. Absolutely absorbed in the moment, we enter a timeless state. We become fascinated and caught up in our creative endeavours; we often speak of 'losing ourselves' within them. In a sense, we do literally lose our selves – dropping our separate sense of identity and merging into the greater flow of life. As Mihaly Csikszentmihalyi, author of *Flow*, says: 'Flow is being completely involved in an activity for its own sake. The ego falls away. Time flies. Every action, movement, and thought follows inevitably from the previous one, like playing jazz.'[60] Entering into the creative flow can be a transcendent and absorbing experience.

Yet finding our way into flow is not always easy, and Surrender doesn't necessarily feel blissful. In fact, often we meet Surrender through challenge, conflict and despair. These feelings act as thresholds, guarding the way to a deeper flow and challenging us to drop the expectations, hopes and fears of the ego in order to step through. In these moments, the experience of Surrender can be both terrifying and exhilarating.

We begin with a goal, a dream, some kind of deep longing. As teams and leaders, our goal might be to return our brand to growth, to become market leader, to launch a new business, or to improve our performance against specific criteria: reducing health-care waiting lists or operation success rates, increasing our school's ranking, improving employee satisfaction. In our personal lives, it could be longing for a new job, for a return to health, for a loving relationship, for reconciliation with a partner or parent, for a new home. In this first stage, we throw ourselves fully into the pursuit of that goal, bringing all our gifts, resources and skills into focus as we head determinedly along the road to success. We set out full of positive intentions, determined to 'make it happen' – a rather dangerous phrase that should alert us immediately to an imminent encounter with Surrender!

Then comes stage two: we hit a wall. This wall can take any number of forms. Maybe despite a brilliant advertising campaign and heavy promotion, our brand continues to decline. Maybe despite a focused search for new clients and projects, our business refuses to grow. Maybe despite our best efforts, change programs fail and employee satisfaction, health-care waiting lists, or the school's ranking remain stagnant. Maybe we don't get the job we wanted, an illness refuses to heal, date after date fails to turn up Mr or Ms Right. It seems that, no matter what we do, we simply cannot achieve our goals and dreams. The strategies that have worked for us in the past simply are not producing the results we hoped for. We have reached the end of the road.

So we enter stage three: we meet our failure with denial or resistance. Digging our heels in, we refuse to acknowledge that our efforts are not working. We keep trying, doing more of the same, hoping that this time we'll get the results we want. So we throw more advertising investment behind a dying brand, we keep meeting with new prospective clients, we keep signing up for the same dating website, we keep trying the same medicine or treatment. Sometimes, determination and persistence do pay off. Yet often what's really needed are different approaches, new actions, deeper changes. As Einstein allegedly said, the definition of insanity is doing the same thing over and over again, and expecting different results.

Often, resistance and denial show up as an ego tantrum. This is the ego's response to its own powerlessness, and just like a toddler's tantrum, it is usually not pretty! Sometimes it rebels with rage, wanting to stamp on everything related to our goal or dream and destroy all the progress we've made in the weeks or months of trying. Sometimes it responds with stubbornness, locking down on its viewpoint and refusing to consider any information, perspective or suggestion that might challenge it. Other times the ego responds by numbing out, burying our goals and dreams under a pervasive sense of boredom or depression. Or it responds with grief, collapsing into despair and spiraling down into a vortex of disempowering negative thoughts that say: *This is too hard; I can't do this; I want to give up; I don't care about this stupid goal or dream anyway.* The challenge in these moments is to turn into Surrender without collapsing into despair. It's true, the ego can't make this move; it is indeed too hard for this narrow part of us, and the ego does need to give up. But some other part of us knows how to find the way through. And it's this part we need to give up into.

Even when we realize we've hit a wall, there's often a fourth stage before we finally turn to Surrender: we try to think our way through the problem. Standing on one side of the river with our dream on the other bank, we try to plan our way across. We try to find the answer and know exactly what path we need to take before we make the first step. We try to figure it all out in our heads, and develop a foolproof to-do list to get us from A to B. We analyse data, create a new five-year plan, detail the steps we will take to improve performance, invest in a failing brand (or a failing economy) because we don't know what else to do. We try harder and harder, desperately hoping that our effort will eventually achieve a breakthrough. Sometimes that works, in the short term at least. More often, it doesn't. In refusing to take bigger risks, to leap into the unknown, to try new approaches, we are led into solutions that are too small. We may patch over the problems with short-term solutions, but we miss the bigger break-throughs, the more radical shifts, the deeper changes. We miss the chance to fundamentally transform ourselves and adapt to our emerging reality. If life were a computer game, we miss the trapdoor that drops us through from Level One into Level Two and beyond.

When we finally stop trying to figure it out with our minds, we move into stage five: Surrender. We stop efforting outwards and we lean into the life emerging from our depths. We accept that we don't know the way forwards, that the certainties we're looking for are not available, that we really don't know how to break through into our emerging future – that, at the most profound level, we don't even know if there is a place for us in that future. And we allow life to show us the way.

Sometimes Surrender happens of its own accord: we go for a walk or a run, or spend time with a friend, and suddenly find ourselves looking at the challenge with new eyes. Other times, we have to engage more consciously with the process of Surrender. This usually begins with the smallest of movements. First, we find a part of our body or being that is not caught up in the fear, grief, rage or resistance, a part that feels open, relaxed and supported. Leaning our awareness into this tiniest sense of comfort, we relax our grip on life. We stop trying to force our way through and open to a sense of something beyond us. Perhaps we notice the beauty of the sky or feel an intangible sense of presence and support in the air around us. Whatever it is, we lean our awareness towards it. From that deeper, more resourceful, more relaxed place, we can then look back at the feelings that are gripping us. We acknowledge them, make space for them, thank them – and continue to lean our awareness towards the sense of peace, comfort and support. Slowly, we melt into this deep sense of well-being. We stop struggling and allow life to carry us wherever it is flowing, through bumpy waters as well as through graceful, easy currents. We find the courage to reclaim Surrender.

The Gifts of Surrender

Nearly all men can stand adversity, but if you want to test a man's character, give him power.

– ABRAHAM LINCOLN

One of the gifts of Surrender is to bring us into a new relationship with power. Instead of seeing power personally, as something to grasp, hold or own, we begin to see it from a more universal perspective – as a current of life moving through us. Myths across time and cultures remind us how important it is to hold power in this lighter, more universal way. In Greek mythology, Cronos, King of the Titans, eats his own children because he is so afraid they will usurp his power when they grow up. Eventually, he is murdered because of these fearful and grasping actions. Modern myths offer us similar warnings, highlighting the danger of grasping at power. Take Darth Vader, seduced by the dark side of the Force. Or Voldemort in the Harry Potter books, whose determination to be powerful and immortal ends up destroying him (and many others along the way). Or Sauron in *The Lord of the Rings*, whose hunger for the Ring of Power leads to war and widespread suffering. Power is seductive, we are warned, and can lead to dangerous and inhumane acts.

In itself, power is not evil or dangerous; it is the way in which we hold it that can make it so. In all these myths, the antagonist seeks power in order to pursue his own agenda, controlling and dominating others in that pursuit. The hero, on the other hand, approaches power with ambivalence. He may have unusual powers: Luke's gift of channelling the Force, Harry's unique ability to survive the killing curse, Frodo's courage and resilience in his journey to destroy the Ring. Yet these powers are held with humility. Often, the hero doesn't even want them. They are simply gifts that he has. And he accepts them and surrenders into the task they lead him to, knowing that whether he likes it or not, it is his destiny.

The *Oxford English Dictionary* definitions of power reinforce these two different approaches. On the one hand, power is defined as 'control or authority over others; dominion, rule; government, command, sway'. In this case, power is tied in to authority, influence, government and rule *over* others. On the other hand, power is 'more generally: ability, capacity'. This second definition is closer to the original source of the word: from the Latin *potere*, meaning 'to be able'.[61] Seen through this second lens, our power has nothing to do with controlling, influencing or directing anyone or anything. It's not power *over*, but power *within*. And we find it not by forcing our way through the world, but by surrendering into the life moving though us.

We get to choose how we hold power in our life and work, and which of these approaches to power we adopt. Myths remind us that we have the potential to be both Harry and Voldemort, Sauron and Frodo, Darth Vader and Luke; both sets of archetypes exist in our inner world. Will we use our position of authority to boost our ego, inflate our own sense of self-worth, subject others to our own agenda and build our own empire? Or will we accept our abilities, embrace our gifts and channel our power into a greater cause: something beyond our own personal gain, our own bank balance, our own promotion? Ultimately, the choice is this: to grasp at power, or to surrender into it, offering our selves and our gifts in service to life.

Unsure of our true answer to these questions, many of us shrink from our own natural power. Sometimes we do this consciously – we push it away, seeing it as ugly, dangerous, corrupt. Other times, we disown power unconsciously, ignoring our gifts and focusing instead on all the ways we feel small, flawed and 'not good enough'. By holding on tightly to a conscious sense of inadequacy, we don't have to look at something even more frightening: our power. Marianne Williamson's often-quoted words capture this tendency to play small and pull away from our magnificence:

> Our deepest fear is not that we are inadequate. Our deepest fear is
> that we are powerful beyond measure. It is our light, not our darkness

that most frightens us. We ask ourselves, Who am I to be brilliant, gorgeous, talented, fabulous? Actually, who are you not to be?[62]

Avoiding our power, we also avoid the temptation to misuse it – to harm others through manipulation, dominion, or uncontrolled outbursts of force, violence or aggression. And we avoid being punished, excluded, abandoned or cast out because others are threatened by our power. After all, history reminds us that we risk attack, imprisonment, torture and even death for stepping into our power. The 'witch' trials of the 15th to 17th centuries are just one example of this. And so we hide behind a forced sense of inadequacy and take refuge in haunting self-doubt: *Am I good enough? Do I deserve this? Am I worthy of this opportunity?* These are painful and uncomfortable questions, but they are safer than confronting the true magnificence of the power that comes through us.

When we surrender, we come into a larger relationship with power, and these questions and doubts become irrelevant. Offering our gifts to life, we no longer need to fear our power or cover it over with a false sense of inadequacy. Enough or not, we simply 'are' – and we offer what we are fully, wholeheartedly and with profound humility. We're not interested in personal power; issues of confidence and self-worth fade out of focus. Instead, we direct our attention to one central question: *How can I serve?* And we live the answer. If that means stepping into responsibility and authority, fine. If it means downsizing our power, that's fine too. As my teacher Brugh Joy said, 'You may be Luke . . . or you may discover you are the grass on which the storm trooper treads.'

One of my clients, Sandeep,[63] followed Surrender into a new relationship with power. Global planning director at a large advertising agency in London, Sandeep was a successful expatriate with a natural sense of humility. Strategically smart, he had progressed easily through the agency. Now, he found himself hitting a wall. He was aware that to be promoted to the next level he would need new skills – the willingness to speak out in meetings and be more 'political'. Yet to Sandeep, stepping into a more public and vociferous role was an act of self-promotion, and he judged it as insincere, lacking in integrity and frankly ugly.

I sensed that Sandeep had hit a wall in his relationship with power, and that he needed a bigger context to frame it in. So in our third or fourth coaching session, I asked him to close his eyes, settle into himself, and see if he could sense the life force in the space around us. After a minute, I noticed his body relax and he began to smile. *What do you feel?* I asked. *I can feel my destiny*, he said. For Sandeep, with his Indian background, 'destiny' was his understanding of the life force that flows through us – of primal creativity. Connecting to this greater source of power, Sandeep surrendered his struggle and stepped into the flow. He no longer needed to repress his natural gifts or powers for fear of becoming pushy or political. He was able to embrace them and follow them into new work – in his case, a career that combined his experience in advertising with his passion for teaching. Reframing his personal power in the context of his destiny, Sandeep came into a natural, safe and easy relationship with power.

Surrendering our gifts back to life, we hold our power lightly, with neither attachment nor fear. We understand that our gifts are something we channel rather than something we own. It is not *our* power, it is the power of life flowing through us. And we offer it back, directing it towards goals and actions that serve and support the bigger story – the unfolding of life on our planet and beyond.

In Service to Life

Thinking only about yourself, fulfilling your immediate wants
and needs, betrays a certain poverty of ambition.
Because it's only when you hitch your wagon to something
larger than yourself that you realize your true potential.

– BARACK OBAMA

Putting service at the core of our organizations and institutions is not a new idea. Theoretically, health care, education, politics and all 'social services' are just that: services to society. Even some of our earliest profit-making businesses strived to be of service. William Hesketh Lever founded Lever Brothers (now Unilever) in the 1890s with an ambition 'to make cleanliness commonplace; to lessen work for women; to foster health and contribute to personal attractiveness, that life may be more enjoyable and rewarding for the people who use our products'.[64] Lever also tried to serve his employees, creating Port Sunlight, a village built specifically for his workers, offering free schools, health care and homes. Similarly, chocolate manufacturers George and Richard Cadbury created the village of Bourneville for their employees with an intention to alleviate the problems of poor, crowded living conditions.[65] Employees were given relatively high salaries, good medical care, spacious homes, access to parks and recreation areas and pioneering pension plans. Integrating service into business missions and practices is not a new concept.

What is new is our understanding of 'service'. In traditional business models, service means addressing the needs of our boss, our customers – and ultimately our shareholders. Fundamentally that means helping them to make money. When we do this well, we get other personal rewards – financial reward, recognition, status, prestige. Through this traditional approach, our serving is centred in a small sense of self (the ego) and those we serve are a disconnected 'other' out there. There is a clear 'giver' and a clear 'receiver'.

One gets to feel good about giving something and helping someone, the other is expected to feel grateful for this act of 'generosity' or 'service'.

In our changing world, new models of business are emerging, grounded in a much wider sense of service. These look beyond our ego needs of survival, recognition and status and towards the deeper needs of our *soul*: to make a difference, have an impact, offer our gifts to something that has meaning for us. Soul-centred service is still anchored in our self – we don't need to abandon our own needs to make a difference – yet it extends out into broader circles that include all those who come into contact with our product or service, directly or indirectly. What's more, making money for ourselves, our customers and our shareholders is simply a by-product of a much bigger intention: to address a fundamental social, economic or environmental problem. In this model of business, definitions of 'giver' and 'receiver' merge, because everyone involved in the business is centred in the same intention, to address the same problem. Some contribute as investors, others as entrepreneurs, others as advisers, others as customers. All roles are equally important and all bring their own rewards. The diagram on the next page shows these two different approaches to service.

When we centre our leadership, businesses and institutions in soul service, we find ourselves on a true path to success. Held together by a common purpose, we discover a natural alignment between customer and client, supplier and retailer, brand team and agency, government and citizen, hospital and patient, one nation and another. This alignment comes from a common intention: to serve life. Centred in this aim, we create generative, collaborative solutions, services and products. The stories in this book are all great examples of this – Innocent, Method, Oprah, Apple, Clif Bar and many other companies whose leaders put their own passions into the service of a wider social need.

The story of the Nest Collective Inc. (Nest) clearly shows this link between success and service. Nest was founded in 2007 by Sheryl O'Loughlin (former CEO of Clif Bar, whose story we explored in

The Circles of Service

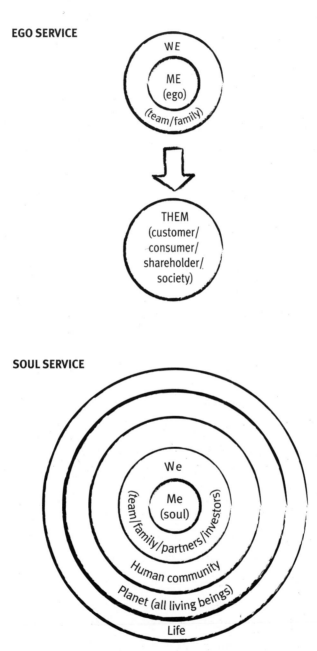

EGO SERVICE

WE

ME
(ego)

(team/family)

THEM
(customer/
consumer/
shareholder/
society)

SOUL SERVICE

We

Me
(soul)

(team/family/partners/investors)

Human community

Planet (all living beings)

Life

chapter 4) and Neil Grimmer. From the start, its intention was to acquire small, values-based organizations and help them grow into large-scale organizations without losing their essence – as Nest puts it, to 'scale with soul'. When they set up Nest in 2007, both founders had recently become parents. Committed to both parenting and career, they struggled to make healthy, homemade food for their kids in their busy lives: 'We were struck by how the food market generally lacked yummy, nourishing, organic food for kids,' Sheryl explains. 'On a more macro scale, we were devastated by the idea that this is the first generation of children who, if current health problems continue at this rate, will die younger than their parents. So we decided to put Nest in service to creating healthy, organic, yummy food for kids.' To get started with that mission, Nest acquired two brands: Plum Organics (simple, organic food for busy babies and toddlers) and Revolution Foods (healthy lunch-box foods for kids).

Setting up Nest was, in part, a self-centred act: it served to make the founders' experience as working parents easier. It emerged from a personal need in their own lives and families. Yet exploring that personal need drew them into a broader experience of service. Nest serves Sheryl and Neil, as co-founders, offering them the inspiration, fulfillment and passion of working for a mission they believe in. It serves its employees, who also get to work for a mission that inspires them. It serves its investors, who can feel good about supporting something that could really make a difference. It serves its local community, bringing vibrancy and opportunity to a previously downtrodden part of town. It serves working parents, who can feel good about feeding their kids healthy food. And of course it serves the kids themselves.

What about the wider community – other species, the planet and life itself? Well, Nest is far from perfect. It works within the same systems as every other contemporary organization and struggles with the same limitations. Yet its explicit intention is to grow towards becoming a sustainable, generative organization, not only for people, but also for the planet. Sheryl speaks to the challenge of this broader sense of service: 'For a company to have a positive impact, it has to serve at all levels – including the planet. Yet the truth is, a truly sustainable organization doesn't exist yet. As a mission-based company, that's frustrating as hell, because we want to be there. Yet every day we face ways we're not there yet – and each one is like a dagger through the heart.' For example, to address the needs of busy parents, Nest's products have to be easy to carry, and just now there are no sustainable packaging options that meet their needs. They are working with packaging partners to find new solutions in the long term. Meanwhile, until those solutions exist, they are simply minimizing their environmental impact, choosing packaging materials that are light and low volume. As Sheryl says, 'We have to surrender: to accept what is, without giving up on what could be. We have to hold the tension between what is and what we want. Because it's in that tension that the most creative, imaginative, innovative solutions magically pop out.'[66]

Nest's story brings us back to the power of Surrender in our journey towards new ways of business in a changing world. Sometimes the ideal solution doesn't exist. Often, we have to grope our way, in the dark, through uncertain, imperfect and conflicted experiences. This is the nature of evolution. Life, too, has had its moments of struggle and confusion, and it too has searched for solutions to evolutionary challenges. Brian Swimme brings one of these moments into focus in his discussion of 'Emergence'. As he explains, at some very early stage in the evolution of the universe, life needed hydrogen. It found a way to get that hydrogen from water, but as the hydrogen was pulled off the water molecules, it released oxygen into the atmosphere. Oxygen is such a powerful element that it became a destructive presence for life, diving into the simple cells that made up life at that stage and tearing them apart. 'Then an amazing moment takes place,' Swimme says. 'The cells found a way to engage with the oxygen – and in that complex process they found a way to live inside one another.'[67] That led to a new, complex eukaryotic cell – a huge evolutionary breakthrough born out of profound challenge.

In a sense, humans are the oxygen of the modern world. We, too, have become extremely powerful, and in many ways damaging and destructive to life because of that power. Yet the solution is not to eradicate us (like the often-cited dinosaurs), or even to eliminate the behaviours that are currently challenging our environment. Take air travel, for example. Yes, we need to think carefully before flying, and yes, we may cut back on unnecessary travel, but eliminating all air travel is most likely not the ultimate solution. After all, the ability to travel and immerse ourselves in different cultures can be immensely valuable, opening our hearts and minds to new ways of serving the world. So rather than collapsing into one side or the other, travelling mindlessly or abolishing air travel completely, we need to sit in the tension of the middle ground between what we need at a personal level and what we need at a planetary level. In that tension, we find the space to discover creative, innovative, sustainable, generative solutions.

This in-between space is often an uncomfortable place to be. As Swimme points out: 'Think of the period in between the moment when oxygen became difficult and when the eukaryote figured out how to deal with it. In that period, life did not know how to proceed. There was a long period of deep, deep, deep, deep ignorance.' The path to success is not signposted in black and white. 'Creative emergence involves groping, involves wandering around, involves profound confusion – involves living with ambiguity and ambivalence. It involves the ability to embrace the situation and not have a clear idea of how to move forwards.'[68]

So, in this particular moment of evolution, what can we surrender into? How might creative emergence unfold through us, and our communities, to address the major challenges of our time? How might it help us re-imagine our schools, hospitals, businesses, politics, agriculture, cities, religions for this changing world? As leaders, organizations and institutions, how might we serve the deeper evolutionary currents of life? We don't need to know the answers – and in fact, most likely, we cannot know the answers. We simply need to surrender into these questions, to offer our creative powers in service to the exploration and discovery of our emerging world.

The stories in this book are filled with such moments of Surrender – times when even the most pioneering leaders didn't know the way forwards, and had to give up control and lean into the natural creativity of life. Innocent's founders couldn't find funding – until one last act of Surrender led them to write an e-mail to their whole address list asking for help. Eric Ryan, founder of Method, had to surrender into the break-up with his girlfriend and the conflict with his boss in order to find the courage to finally pursue his dream. Scott Eberle had to surrender the need to have all the answers and work with the minimal facts about HIV available at the time.

In a sense, Surrender is the path through any journey of change. Sometimes we surrender into Dying, letting go of habits, beliefs, identities, systems and structures that do not belong in our emerging world. Sometimes we surrender into the Stillness, tolerating the discomfort of the Threshold. Sometimes we surrender to our Intuition, listening quietly for what wants to emerge. Sometimes we surrender into our Wildness, moving beyond the old rules and leaning into what brings us alive. Sometimes we surrender into Vulnerability, giving ourselves to the wide range of emotions that arise in times of change. Within every journey of change, it is Surrender that guides us fiercely and gently towards our emerging world. It is Surrender that brings us into a deeper sense of service, realigning our leadership, businesses and institutions around the shifting currents and longings of life.

So, we loop around to where we started this conversation in Chapter 1. Surrendering into Dying brings us to new life; surrendering into life brings us to more Dying, and the cycle begins again. The journey of change is a circular journey, in which we never 'arrive'. We simply deepen into our soul and into the natural evolutionary journey of the universe, of which we are a small and valuable part. And with each cycle, we courageously offer more of our wild self and its gifts in service to the bigger story: the journey of life.

SURRENDER AS A PATH TO LEADERSHIP

Surrendering to Illness – and Beyond
Casey's Story

The daughter of two alcoholic parents, Casey grew up in a chaotic and unpredictable home where she learned that in order to survive she needed to stay in control, always. That was how she lived her life, right up until the age of 50. Driven, ambitious, efficient, she knew that when she set her will towards something, she could always achieve it. Her motto was 'Impossible is nothing!' and she applied it to every challenge she encountered, in her personal and working life.

By the age of 50, Casey was a career wonder woman. She ran her own business, consulting in cultural diversity, working with high-powered clients in large multinationals. She was also a university lecturer for various MBA programs, taught online, served as president of a large professional women's network and on the board of a prestigious Chamber of Commerce, and became known as a global expert in her field. Working 70-hour weeks, she described herself as the Energizer Bunny – capable, energetic, someone who never got ill and certainly never needed help. Surrender was not part of her vocabulary.

That all changed in 2007. One morning, Casey woke up to discover that her whole body was numb. Within a week, she was in intensive care, paralysed from her head to her chest. She was diagnosed with Guillain-Barré syndrome, an auto-immune illness in which the nervous system attacks itself, leading to partial paralysis and severe nerve pain – as she described it, 'feeling that 10,000 pins are being stuck into you.' Because of the paralysis in her face, she couldn't see, eat or speak, and as the illness spread down her body it became increasingly hard to breathe. The doctors had no idea how long the symptoms would last or even whether she would recover at all. The best they could say was 'it'll probably be all right'.

Casey hit a wall. Unable to work because of her illness, she saw her identity as career superwoman begin to crumble. Still, she refused to acknowledge the severity of her illness and pushed on in resistance and denial. At the very first signs of improvement, she invited 12 people to come and stay, reassuring them it was 'business as normal'. It was at the end of that weekend that she finally surrendered. Exhausted, she broke down and cried for the first time since she'd become ill. 'It was that moment that I finally accepted I was really ill. I also knew that I couldn't solve this problem with any of my usual strategies – rationalizing it, formulating a plan, pushing through and being tough and independent. I needed to learn to ask for help. That was something I had never done before, and I was terrified.'

So Casey finally turned towards Surrender. Seeking out help, she got in touch with me and set up a series of coaching sessions. At first, in those sessions, she mostly vented her outrage and sense of injustice. It wasn't fair. She didn't understand. How long was this going to last? What could she do to make it better? Giving space to the feelings of rage, she slowly began to dig down behind the anger towards deeper vulnerabilities. There was exhaustion, grief, loss, powerlessness, longing to be taken care of, loneliness. And beyond all these feelings – hope for a different kind of life. As she stopped resisting the experience, Casey began to see how powerlessness might initiate her into new ways of being, shifting her from her driven, high-achieving lifestyle into a more gentle, open, receptive way of being in the world.

Letting go of old expectations and plans, Casey began to restructure her life around this new, receptive approach to life. She moved back from Holland to a cabin in rural Canada, ended a 30-year marriage, and began to reclaim her body and her sexuality. Letting go of career wonder woman, she closed her consultancy practice and focused exclusively on her work as a university professor, offering online courses that she could teach from her home. These were difficult decisions and they involved sacrifice. Yet as she made them, despite the grief and guilt, she felt a sense of peace. Surrendering to these changes, she came back into alignment with her soul and with life – and slowly began to recover physically.

Even after the illness passed, Surrender continued to run through Casey's life and work. After initiating her divorce and cutting back her workload, she found herself short of money. So she meditated and asked for help. That act of Surrender dropped her into the creative flow and carried her towards an unexpected opportunity. The next day, she got an e-mail from a university in Holland that she hadn't worked with for years, asking if she had experience in online learning and, if so, whether she'd be willing to help them develop an online program. It was a project that fitted her skills and passion completely, with the potential to serve others. It was also well paid and perfectly timed to co-ordinate with a trip she had already planned to Holland – the perfect solution to her financial worries.

Casey's experience with Surrender was painful, difficult, frightening – and life-changing. Her illness forced her to question the way she was approaching her life and work. It gently (and sometimes not so gently) encouraged her to make changes, to grow and evolve in her inner and outer world. Ultimately, by surrendering to the challenges and uncertainty of illness, she found her way through into new success and a new way of being in the world.

Source: My interview and coaching sessions with Casey.
I have changed my client's name in order to protect her privacy.

PRACTICE # 6

Ceremony

Ceremony is a way of uniting our personal power with the greater powers of the universe. All cultures have formal ceremonies, passed down through the generations: Native American vision quests, bar mitzvahs, christenings, marriages, funerals and other rituals that mark the major transitions through different life stages and experiences. Alongside these formal ceremonies, we can also create our own simple, everyday ceremonies. Their purpose is to symbolically enact where we are now – and then open us to receive guidance on where we might go next. In the words of Rumi's poem 'Zero Circle', we are saying, 'with tremendous eloquence, Lead us!'

The framework of a ceremony includes the following elements:

1. Begin with an **intention** – what are you marking with this ceremony? What question do you hope to receive guidance on?

2. **Prepare** for the ceremony. You might spend five minutes doing this, five days, five weeks, five months or longer, depending on the nature of the ceremony you are about to step into. Preparing for the ceremony might include gathering objects that will feature in it. For example, if you're letting go of an old job or relationship, you may include a photo or object that represents that experience or phase of your life. You may also want to think about what you'll wear, what a good location for your ceremony might be, who else might be there (if anyone), what time of day would be most appropriate and other details of the ceremony. In planning these details, keep your intention in mind, and ensure that every detail supports that intention.

3. When it's time for the ceremony itself, **open the space**. You can do that by marking a threshold, playing a piece of music, lighting a candle, or any other symbolic act that says: 'This ceremony is beginning.' You may want to state your intention out loud.

4. **Let the ceremony do you.** You may have all kinds of plans for how the ceremony will unfold. Set them aside. Open to the space, and listen deeply to let it move you through the experience. Follow your inner guidance about when it's time to move, where to go, what to do and what to say. Trust yourself and your instincts completely, and engage with whatever shows up.

5. Find a way to **enact your experience**. For example, if you're ready to let go of something, you may want to burn, break, smash or bury an object to symbolically enact that readiness. If you're ready to open to something new, you may want to lie with your arms and heart open, or create a container to receive the new life. There are no right and wrongs – just trust your own heart.

6. When the ceremony feels done (or when the time you've set aside for it is complete), **close the space**. Here, you may like to state out loud what you've discovered and what (if anything) you're ready to commit to. How you end the ceremony depends on how you opened it. If you lit a candle when you opened the ceremony, blow it out; if you crossed a threshold, go back to that place and cross it in the other direction; if you arranged a space for your ceremony, dismantle it.

7. As you move back into your everyday reality, **stay open**. Keep the experience of your ceremony alive within you – perhaps by re-reading any journal entries from that time, listening to a certain piece of music, revisiting art you created during the ceremony, or using anything that featured in your ceremony (a leaf, a shell, a feather) as a touchstone. Notice what might have changed or

shifted through the ceremony. Stay particularly open to synchronicities and seemingly chance encounters over the next few weeks: these might be a response to your ceremonial intention.

Some Last Words

And so we come to the end – or perhaps to the beginning.

Coming to the end myself, I'm struck by how much is left unsaid. There are of course other forgotten paths to leadership – other shadow qualities like Play, Love, Collaboration, Trust and Intimacy to reclaim. But for now, these six paths are enough.

I hope these words have moved or stirred you in some way. Perhaps they have reminded you of some truths that you know, but had forgotten – about your self, your leadership, your work or even Life itself.

Engaging your own journey of transformation is not an easy task. It requires energy, risk, commitment, willingness to be lost, courage to stray from the conventional path and to head, over and over, into the wildness of your heart. I'd like to say that it leads you to some kind of nirvana, where everything falls into place, where life is easy and sweet and successful every moment of every day. Yet, from what I've seen, it doesn't generally work that way! Life is always evolving, always mysterious, always leading us to our edge, so that we can grow and transform into the next layer of our potential – and so always filled with challenges.

Even so, there are great rewards from this journey. As we grow into these forgotten aspects of life and leadership, we discover more of our self. We bring more of our gifts into our leadership and work. We have a greater impact on the world we live in. We start to feel that we are living the life we were born to live – living what is uniquely ours to be and to discover. We come more alive. Living our life from our centre, there is a new ground, a new sense of purpose and security that comes from deep within, which guides and comforts us through the inevitable challenges and difficulties.

There are also gifts to the wider society and system. These are perhaps harder to identify and measure yet we can intuitively sense them. We catch a glimpse of them in the stories and case studies of the pioneering leaders who followed this journey of transformation to address not only personal needs, but also the needs of wider communities, systems and ecosystems. As more and more leaders take this journey of self-discovery to find their true place in the world, we reach a 'tipping point' where the whole system responds – leading, eventually, to a more vital, creative, healthy and sustainable human presence on the planet.

If you feel inspired to move towards the changes stirring in your heart or your life – do it. If you know where to start – great. If not, start where you are. Take just five minutes each morning to sit in silence and listen intuitively for one thing you can do that day to move towards your wild self. Then take that step . . . and let the journey unfold.

You might like to check out the workshops and tele-classes on www.wildcourage.com that are designed to support and guide you through your own journey of change. Or perhaps tap into the online community to share your stories and witness others' experiences. Feel free, too, to reach out by e-mail: stories@wildcourage.com. I'd love to hear your stories, and how this book may have shaped, supported or influenced you. No matter where you are, know that you are not alone.

May you find the courage to step into your journey of transformation. And may that courage serve you, your people, the planet and Life, carrying us forwards into a rich and sustainable future.

And if our paths cross, I look forward to meeting you and witnessing your story!

Acknowledgments

So many people made the writing of this book possible, and I am grateful to each of you for your support, encouragement, belief and inspiration. First, my teachers: those who opened me to my own journey of change and new ways of seeing the world – Anup, Sandra Gonzalez, Liz Alcalay, Brugh Joy, Hal and Sidra Stone, David Whyte, Brian Swimme, Kerry Brady, Sandra Ingerman, Meredith Little, Scott Eberle and my mentor, cheerleader and friend Carolyn Conger.

I'm grateful to all my friends, for their tireless support and enthusiasm, and for the endless conversations about the title that they had to put up with! To my family, for their love and encouragement, and for teaching me that anything is possible. To my clients, whose stories, struggles and successes touch, open and inspire me every day. To Adam Morgan, one of my early champions, whose enthusiasm and courage to recommend my work has led to so many interesting clients. To Bonnie and Pam, for opening me to my tribe in California and for always welcoming me so fully into your hearts and lives. And to Jim Marsden and Kate Franklin for your friendship and companionship, in work and beyond.

Then, in the writing of the book itself. To Dan, Mic, Penny, Jim, David, Dad – my first readers – for your encouragement and comments, and for helping me believe in those early seeds of the idea. To Tim Koogle, for your generous offer to write the Foreword, and for patiently reading through draft after draft to make that happen. To Pip, for the beautiful photos. To all the leaders I interviewed, for taking time to share your inspiring and powerful stories. To Dorothy Chitty and Richard Dodman, who led me to my agent, Jane Graham Maw – and to Jane, for first believing in me and for your tireless help in drafting and redrafting the proposal. To my publisher, Michael Mann, for your vision and encouragement, and for staying in the conversation through all the ups and downs. To the team at Watkins and

Sterling, whose job is just beginning. To Scott Eberle, for your incredible generosity and for the courageous feedback that helped strengthen the early drafts into something readable. Last, and in no way least, to Anne Barthel, my New York editor, for turning the loneliness of writing into a shared experience, for the laughter, commitment, patience, vision and encouragement and for your amazing ability to pay attention to the tiniest detail and the biggest picture. I could not have hoped for a better editor.

Finally – to you, my reader, without whom this book would not exist.

Notes

Introduction

1 *Biodiversity in the Next Millennium,* a 1998 survey of 400 biologists conducted by New York's American Museum of Natural History. American Museum of Natural History Press Release, 20 April 1998, http://www.well.com/~davidu/amnh.html

2 World Health Organization report. http://www.who.int/mental_health/prevention/suicide/suicideprevent/en/index.html.

3 Hale, A. 1997, 'ABC of Mental Health: Depression', *British Medical Journal,* 315, 5 July 1997, pp. 43–46

Chapter 1

4 Steve Jobs, commencement address (2005) quoted in *Stanford Report* (14 June 2005). The full transcript of this speech is available online: http://news-service.stanford.edu/news/2005/june15/jobs-061505.html.

5 Johann Wolfgang von Goethe, 'The Holy Longing', *Selected Poetry,* translated by David Luke, Penguin Classics, London, 2005

6 I'm grateful to Scott Eberle, Meredith Little and the School of Lost Borders for introducing me to this ancient tradition.

Chapter 2

7 *Oxford English Dictionary* definition of 'quantum vacuum'.

8 Brian Swimme, *The Universe Is a Green Dragon: A Cosmic Creation Story,* Bear & Co., Rochester, VT, 2001. pp. 37-38.

9 Paul Davies, *The Last Three Minutes: Speculating about the Fate of the Cosmos* (Science Masters), originally published by Weidenfeld & Nicholson, London, 1994, pb edition by Phoenix, an imprint of Orion Books Ltd, London, 1995, re-issued 2001.

10 Nyoshul Khen Rinpoche from 'Natural Great Peace' text by Sogyal Rinpoche, Tertön Sogyal Trust, 2009. http://www.rigpa.org/en/teachings/extracts-of-articles-and-publications.

11 Nikola Tesla (1856–1943) quoted in the *New York Times* by Orrin E. Dunalp Jr in 'Tesla sees evidence that radio and light are sound', *New York Times,* 8 April, 1934, p.9, col 1.

12 Rachael Kessler, *The Soul of Education: Helping Students Find Connection, Compassion, and Character at School,* Association for Supervision and Curriculum Development (ASCD), Alexandria, VA, 2000.

13 Andrew Simms, Anna Coote & Jane Franklin, '21 Hours: Why a shorter working week can help us all to flourish in the 21st Century', *New Economic Forum*, February 2010.

14 *Oxford English Dictionary* definition of 'productivity'.

15 *Oxford English Dictionary* definition of 'productiveness'.

Chapter 3

16 I have changed the name to protect Mary's privacy.

17 Carl Jung, *The Portable Jung*, ed. Joseph Campbell, Penguin, 1971. p.271.

18 Erik Dane & Michael G. Pratt, 'Exploring Intuition and its Role in Managerial Decision Making' in *Academy of Management Review*, 2007, Volume 32, No. 1. p.35.

19 *Oxford English Dictionary*, definition of 'soul'.

20 Richard Tarnas, *The Passion of the Western Mind: Understanding the Ideas that Have Shaped Our World View*, Pimlico, London, 1991, p.10.

21 Carl Jung, 'Psychological Types' in *The Portable Jung*, ed. Joseph Campbell, Penguin, 1971. p.261.

22 Carl Jung, 'Psychological Types' in *The Portable Jung*, ed. Joseph Campbell, Penguin, 1971. p.220.

23 Carl Jung, 'Psychological Types' in *The Portable Jung*, ed. Joseph Campbell, Penguin, 1971. p.222.

24 Steve Jobs, commencement address (2005) quoted in *Stanford Report*, 14 June 2005 (http://news-service.stanford.edu/news/2005/june15/jobs-061505.html).

25 Steve Jobs, commencement address (2005) quoted in *Stanford Report*, 14 June 2005 (http://news-service.stanford.edu/news/2005/june15/jobs-061505.html).

26 See http://www.myersbriggs.org/ for more about Myers Briggs Personality Types.

27 *Oxford English Dictionary*, definition of 'symbol (n)'.

28 http://www.mindpowernews.com/BrilliantDreams.htm

29 Mary Wollstonecraft Shelley, *Frankenstein: Or the Modern Prometheus*, from the preface to the 1831 edition originally published by Henry Colburn and Richard Bentley, Penguin Popular Classics, Penguin Books Ltd, London, 2007.

30 http://www.mindpowernews.com/BrilliantDreams.htm

31 Paul Strathern, *Mendeleyev's Dream: The Quest for the Elements* , Penguin, 2001.

32 http://www.mindpowernews.com/BrilliantDreams.htm; *A Popular History of American Invention*, Waldemar Kaempffert, Vol 2, p.385, Scribner, NY.

33 Dr. James Lovelock, excerpt from a panel discussion with young people organized by the Goi Peace Foundation on 26 November, 2000, at the Tokyo American Club

while James Lovelock was in Japan to accept the Goi Peace Award 2000. http://www.goipeace.or.jp/english/activities/award/award2-1.html. Goi Peace Foundation Report, 1999–2000, p.18. http://www.intuition-in-service.org.

34   Ward Hill Lamon, James A. Rawley & Dorothy Lamon Teillard, *Recollections of Abraham Lincoln*, originally published in 1895. Reprint of 1911 edition edited by Dorothy Lamon Teillard, introduced by James A. Rawley, University of Nebraska Press, Lincoln, NE, 1994. Chapter VII, pp.114–18.

Chapter 4

35   The Environmental Literacy Council, 'How many species are there?' http://www.enviroliteracy.org/article.php./58.html

36   *Oxford English Dictionary*, definition of 'wild'.

37   John Taylor Gatto, quoting Cubberly as writing in his Columbia Teachers' College Dissertation of 1905, *The Underground History of American Education: An Intimate Investigation into the Problem of Modern Schooling*. Oxford Village Press, NY, 2001

38   Oprah Winfrey, commencement speech, Stanford, June 2008. http://news.stanford.edu/news/2008/june18/como-061808.html.

39   J.K. Rowling, Harvard 2008 commencement speech. 'The Fringe Benefits of Failure and the Importance of Imagination', published in *Harvard Magazine*, June 5, 2008. http://harvardmagazine.com/commencement/the-fringe-benefits-failure-the-importance-imagination.

40   From a talk by Zarine Kharas at the RSA, London, 22 April 2009.

41   Jim Collins, *Good to Great: Why Some Companies Make the Leap and Others Don't*, Random House Business Books, London, 2001.

42   Oprah Winfrey, commencement speech, Stanford, June, 2008. http://news.stanford.edu/news/2008/june18/como-061808.html.

43   Brian Swimme, *The Powers of the Universe* (DVD), 'Transformation & Transmutation'.

44   Mihaly Csíkszentmihílyi, *Flow: The Psychology of Optimal Experience*, Harper Perennial Modern Classics, HarperCollins, London, 2008.

45   Brian Swimme, *The Powers of the Universe* (DVD), 'Transmutation'.

Chapter 5

46   I have changed my client's name to respect her privacy.

47   Robert Payne, *The Life and Death of Adolf Hitler*, New York, New York: Hippocrene Books, 1990, p.22.

48   Adolf Hitler, *Mein Kampf*. http://www.hitler.org/writings/Mein_Kampf/mkv1ch02.html

49   Adolf Hitler, *Mein Kampf*.
     http://www.hitler.org/writings/Mein_Kampf/mkv1ch02.html

50   Quote from my interview with Richard Hytner, Deputy Chairman, Saatchi & Saatchi.

51   Joanna Macy, 'The Greatest Danger', *Yes!* Magazine, 1 February 2008.

52   *New York Times* article 'As China Roars, Pollution Reaches Deadly Extremes', August 26 2007, which cites studies by The World Bank and environmental agency SEPA and by The World Health Organization.

53   DVD *The Corporation*, a film by Mark Achbar, Joanna Abbott and Joel Bachan. http://www.thecorporation.com.

54   Interface's website. www.interfaceglobal.com/Sustainability

55   Joanna Macy, 'The Greatest Danger', *Yes!* Magazine, 1 February, 2008.

Chapter 6

56   Brian Swimme interview with Susan Bridle, 'Comprehensive Compassion', in *What Is Enlightenment*, Spring-Summer 2001.
     (http://www.enlightennext.org/magazine/j19/swimme.asp?page=2)

57   Brian Swimme, *The Powers of the Universe* (DVD), 'Emergence'.

58   Rumi, Jalal Al-Din, 'The Guest House', from *Say I am You: Poetry Interspersed with Stories of Rumi and Shams*, translated by John Moyne and Coleman Barks, Thomas Shore Inc., 1994.

59   Brian Swimme, *The Powers of The Universe* (DVD)

60   Mihaly Csikszentmihalyi, *Flow: The Psychology of Optimal Experience*, Harper Perennial Modern Classics, HarperCollins, London, 2008.

61   *Oxford English Dictionary* definition of 'power'.

62   Marianne Williamson, *A Return to Love: Reflections on the Principles of* A Course in Miracles, HarperCollins, NY, 1992. pp.190–191.

63   I have changed my client's name to respect his privacy.

64   http://www.unilever.com/aboutus/ourhistory/

65   www.cadbury.co.uk

66   From interviews with Sheryl O'Loughlin, CEO of the Nest Collective Inc, and Neil Grimmer, Chief Innovation Officer.

67   Brian Swimme interview with Susan Bridle, 'Comprehensive Compassion', in *What Is Enlightenment*, Spring-Summer 2001.
     (http://www.enlightennext.org/magazine/j19/swimme.asp?page=2)

68   Brian Swimme, *The Powers of the Universe* (DVD), 'Emergence'.

Bibliography and References

The author and publisher would like to thank all those who have given permission to reproduce material protected by copyright. Every effort has been made to secure permission for such material and will be pleased to make good any omissions brought to their attention in future printings of this book.

Alda, Alan, 62nd Commencement Speech, Connecticut College, 1980

Anderson, Ray, quoted in *The Corporation*, a film by Mark Achbar, Joanna Abbott and Joel Bachan. http://www.thecorporation.com.

Bridges, William, *Transitions: Making Sense of Life's Changes*, revised 25th anniversary edition, Da Capo Press, Cambridge, MA, 2004

Campbell, Joseph, *The Hero with a Thousand Faces*, first published in 1949, new edition as part of the *Collected Works of Joseph Campbell*, Joseph Campbell Foundation and New World Library, Novato, CA, 2008

Collins, Jim, *Good to Great: Why Some Companies Make the Leap and Others Don't*, Random House Business Books, London, 2001

Cummings, E. E. , 'A Poet's Advice to Students', first published as a letter to high school students at Ottawa Hills High School, *E. E. Cummings, a Miscellany* (1st ed.). Edited, with an introduction and notes, by George J. Firmage. Argophile Press, New York , 1958

Csíkszentmihílyi, Mihaly, *Flow: The Psychology of Optimal Experience*, Harper Perennial Modern Classics, HarperCollins, London, 2008

Davies, Paul, *The Last Three Minutes: Speculating about the Fate of the Cosmos* (Science Masters), Phoenix (an imprint of Orion Books Ltd), London, 1995

Dunalp, Orrin E. Jr., 'Tesla sees evidence that radio and light are sound', *New York Times*, 8 April, 1934

Eliot, T. S., 'Little Gidding, V' from *Four Quartets: Collected Poems 1909–62*, Faber and Faber, London, 2002

Gennep, Arnold van, *Les Rites de Passage*, Emile Noury, Paris, 1909. English translation by Monika Vizedom and Gabrielle L. Caffee, *The Rites of Passage*, Chicago Press, Chicago, IL, 1960

Goethe, Johann Wolfgang von, 'The Holy Longing', *Selected Poetry*, translated by David Luke, Penguin Classics, London, 2005

Hitler, Adolf, *Mein Kampf*, http://www.hitler.org/writings/Mein_Kampf/mkv1ch02.html

Kessler, Rachael, *The Soul of Education: Helping Students Find Connection, Compassion, and Character at School*, Association for Supervision and Curriculum Development (ASCD), Alexandria, VA, 2000

Lamon, Ward Hill, *Recollections of Abraham Lincoln*, originally published in 1895. Reprint of 1911 edition edited by Dorothy Lamon Teillard, introduced by James A. Rawley, University of Nebraska Press, Lincoln, NE, 1994

Lao Tzu, *Tao Te Ching*, trans. D. C. Lau, Penguin Books, London, 2009

Lawrence, D. H. (a letter by D. H. Lawrence to Mabel Dodge Luhan, 19 September 1924), *The Letters of D. H. Lawrence*, Volume 1924–1927, The Cambridge Edition, edited by James T. Boulton and Lindeth Vasey, Cambridge University Press, Cambridge, 1989

L'Engle, Madeleine, *Walking on Water: Reflections on Faith and Art*, The Wheaton Library Series, H. Shaw, Wheaton, IL, 1980, 2000

Nietzsche, Friedrich, *Thus Spoke Zarathustra: A Book For Everyone And No One*, Trans. R. J. Hollingdale, Penguin Classic, London, 1974

Obama, Barack, Commencement Address at Wesleyan University, Middletown, Connecticut, USA, 28 May, 2000

Rinpoche, Sogyal, quoting Nyoshul Khen Rinpoche in *Natural Great Peace*, Tertön Sogyal Trust, 2009

Rumi, *Say I Am You: Poetry Interspersed with Stories of Rumi and Shams*, translated by John Moyne and Coleman Barks. Printed and bound by Thomas Shore Inc, Dexter Michigan, 1994.

Scott Peck, M., *The Different Drum: Community-Making and Peace*, Touchstone (Simon & Schuster), New York, 1988

Shelley, Mary Wollstonecraft, *Frankenstein: Or the Modern Prometheus*, Penguin Popular Classics, Penguin Books Ltd, London, 2007

Stacey, Ralph, *Complexity and Creativity in Organizations*, Berrett-Koehler, San Francisco, 1996

Swimme, Brian, *The Universe Is a Green Dragon: A Cosmic Creation Story*, Bear & Co., Rochester, VT, 2001

Tarnas, Richard, *The Passion of the Western Mind: Understanding the Ideas that Have Shaped Our World View*, Pimlico, London, 1991

Tolle, Eckhart, *Stillness Speaks*, New World Library, Novato, CA, 2003

Whitman, Walt, *Leaves of Grass*, quoted in *The Oxford Book of American Essays*, Matthews, Brander, ed., Oxford University Press, NY, 1914

Williamson, Marianne, *A Return to Love: Reflections on the Principles of A Course in Miracles*, HarperCollins, NY, 1992